American Christianity

DIVINE & NAKED

Matthew Pennock

For Jesus, the Founder and Perfecter of our Faith.
Special thanks to James Taplin, Chris Ratzlaff, Charles Meeker,
Jeremiah Duncan, Grant Conley, and Bradley Wilson for all their
help and thoughtful feedback.

Is this the city that was called
the perfection of beauty,
the joy of all the earth?
Lam. 2:15

Better is a little with the fear of the Lord
than great treasure and trouble with it.
Proverbs 15:16

Contents

Introduction

What is "American Christianity"? A divine plan of our age? A whorish prostitute? A lost cause? With this book I want to answer that though it has been encumbered in whorish activity it is not a lost cause. The Church of America is divine and has a set-apart purpose. It is just as divine as the Church in any other nation or people group. That aside, it must be known that the label itself defines a broad spectrum of things. It should be looked at as the spiritual undercurrent of the Christian community in America and far from anything formal or official. Neither is it limited to the political confines of the U.S.A., but in fact reflects a world of Christianity in which America seems to be at the epicenter.

As American power cannot be circumvented on this earth, neither can this "American Christianity". Despite the fact that American Christians only occupy a tiny slice of the world's Christian population (perhaps only 5%), the power and thrust of it is truly staggering. It is everywhere, it is huge, and it is powerful. Even now as the American Christian community is in decline and the center of Christian missions is shifting to other nations, the effects remain deep and widespread.

In ten years of traveling and ministering around the world I have noticed that the American Church seems to endure more mockery than any other national church. This is our main form of persecution. This may come as a surprise to you or it may not. If you are attuned to scriptures such as Psalm 79:4, *"We have become a taunt to our neighbors, mocked and derided by those around us."* or Lamentations 1:7, *"Jerusalem remembers in the days of her affliction and wandering all the precious things that were hers from days of old. When her people fell into the hand of the foe, and there was none to help her, her foes gloated over her; they mocked at her downfall.* " then you might have an idea of where our church stands at this point in time.

Our days are surely not like the days of old—when the church was a fearsome place according to Acts 5:12, *"None of the rest dared join them, but the people held them in high esteem."* Somewhere along the line the power and boldness of the Church was lost, and today the Church is so mocked that the mockery has nearly become an enterprise. Gloated over day after day, it's almost impossible to miss: cartoons, advertisements, souvenirs, TV, radio, newspapers, magazines, tabloids, movies, comics, posters, bumper stickers, and the list goes on and on. It is an enormous amount of gloat for a religion. But it doesn't stop there; the Church finds itself gloated over even from within. I have heard it in the mission field, in local churches, in bible colleges, and even in the ranks of leadership. It is difficult to find such a lack of honor and respect in other religions. Yet we should never be dismayed at this. For, *"If you were of the world, the world would love you as its own; but because you are not of the world, but I chose you out of the world, therefore the world hates you."*[1]

The pierce of all this comes when we understand why the Bride is so mocked. *"Jerusalem sinned grievously,"* says Jeremiah in Lamentations 1:8, *"therefore she became filthy; all who honored her despise her, for they have seen her nakedness; she herself groans and turns her face away."* This old tale of Jerusalem's exile prophetically speaks a truth for us which is being repeated in this very hour. It is because of her downfall.

---

[1] John 15:19

In the previous verse Jeremiah notes, *"…her foes gloated over her; they mocked at her downfall."*

We could easily quote a multitude of preachers this last century prophetically calling out to the Church that she is in a downfall. J. Vernon McGee said he could quote a hundred himself. It is no mystery anymore that she has fallen into a wallowing state. So is it any wonder that the once majestic bride who made her entrance into the world by fearsome power and beauty—so that historians who wrote about the early church were amazed at her—is now exceedingly mocked as she is counted as a naked left-over and a "has-been"? How could you not mock at such a sight? How lonely sits the city that was once full of people. Distressed, mourning, weeping, mocked, widowed.

But there is still hope! The downfall is the sin, and Christ has made a way to reverse it all! If a corporate repentance for the sinfulness were to take place, then and only then as one of our most beloved verses declare, *"if my people who are called by my name humble themselves, and pray and seek my face and turn from their wicked ways, then I will hear from heaven and will forgive their sin and heal their land."*[2]

Let us follow Daniel's example as he and his people were in exile, *"O Lord, hear; O Lord, forgive. O Lord, pay attention and act. Delay not, for your own sake, O my God, because your city and your people are called by your name."* [3] The time is now to turn aside from our church rituals and programs for a moment and give ourselves together to praying and seeking God's face and turning from our wickedness and disobedience.

---

[2] 2 Chronicles 7:14
[3] Daniel 9:19

Maybe you like America, maybe you don't. It has its delightful sides and its dark sides. Jesus came not to condemn or judge and we need to be like him. I love a lot of things about America and its church. There are also things that grieve me. But it is not for me to judge, but only to warn, even as Jesus warned certain cities.[4] The Holy Spirit teaches us to be impartial toward people, and therefore we need to love all people the same. My culture and race is no better than any other and vice versa. Let us stand firm upon the Solid Rock which cannot be shaken. All nations in this world including America, can, and will be shaken. This book invites you, whether you follow Jesus or not, to think upon his words in regards to the cloud of confusion we so often find ourselves in when we think about the culture and ways of the wealthiest and most powerful nation that has ever existed on earth.

For those of us who have picked up the cross-bound course after our predecessors we must make a choice as to how we will continue in it. Some have chosen the choking cares of the world, some have chosen to live for themselves, and some have chosen to compromise everything. But who will choose to endure with the Lord Jesus Christ to the end? May our eyes not be stuck on the worries or short-comings of the country and the church which we are a part of. After all, there is nothing new under the sun—what happens here has happened before in other civilizations. Rather, may our eyes be steadfastly fixed upon heaven and the upward call of God in Christ Jesus!

---

[4] Mattherw 11:21

The Great City

"If there is a global civilization, it is American. Nor is it just McDonald's and Hollywood, it is also Microsoft and Harvard. Wealthy Romans used to send their children to Greek universities; today's Greeks, that is, the Europeans, send their kids to Roman, that is, American, universities."

Josef Joffe, Die Zeit editor

"I sought for the greatness of the United States in her commodious harbors, her ample rivers, her fertile fields, and boundless forests--and it was not there. I sought for it in her rich mines, her vast world commerce, her public school system, and in her institutions of higher learning--and it was not there. I looked for it in her democratic Congress and her matchless Constitution--and it was not there. Not until I went into the churches of America and heard her pulpits flame with righteousness did I understand the secret of her genius and power. America is great because America is good, and if America ever ceases to be good, America will cease to be great!"

French writer Alexis de Tocqueville, after visiting America in 1831

You stare at a some pieces of paper in your hand in bewilderment, but it's not the first time. For weeks you have wandered in mind in imaginative contemplation over these pieces of paper. "Destination: Great City" it reads. You have heard so much about this place since your youth, and you've always heard your neighbors boasting about how they will someday go there or wishing they could. But you have the papers now, and the rest can only shake their heads in disbelief that you could have won such a highly prized 'lottery'. It's so difficult to obtain the necessary documents to enter that city, that most people who try never even get close. The requirements are so stringent that those who do make it are considered lucky or wealthy.

It is a city known for its business and innovation. The people constitute only 5 percent of the world's population, yet its influence reaches to the farthest corners of the earth. So much of your own society and lifestyle had its origins in the Great City. It's hard to imagine how your society would get on without it, for there is quite a bit of established reliance on them. It's seems that everything takes its example from the Great City—your own politicians mimic policies from theirs; their science and technology is incorporated into your own engineering technology and educational curriculum; their religious leaders tend to be the role models and authoritative figures from which your own religious leaders get their dogma. So much depends on them. Despite its population, the city has utterly overshadowed the rest of the world in military strength, political prowess, technology, science, and economics. Money flows in a blur; incalculable in amount. Indeed, how great it would be to go there and experience in the flesh the life, the sounds, the wisdom, the superiority, the beauty, and the strength. Of all the cities in the world you could visit, this one makes for a most prized ornament on your desk. A boast for life. During the flight on the airplane which was itself a product of this civilization, you count the hours and anxieties. Your stomach turns with the kind of anticipation of a young child going to Disneyland.

***

For a great majority of the people of the world today, that 'great city' is known as America. Many times have I sat on an airplane next to such a person on their first visit to America. The world has not seen such a 'city' since the days of Rome. No country is more talked about, written about, or watched than America. Much of the world is found to be more informed of its happenings than those who live in it. It is truly a 'great' city in every sense of the word. For from here came a lot into the world: the car, internet, telephones, movies, electricity. And what is even more astounding is that it all came in a just a little more than a hundred years. From the perspective of the outsider, America is a prodigy at the least.

In a sense, Christianity has also largely come from here–that is in its present day form. America has sent out the most missionaries in all of history numbering the hundreds of thousands, not to mention the global broadcasting of Christian television and radio which directly influences or impacts nearly every country. As a result, Christianity with an American 'taint' can be seen just about anywhere. Deep in the bush in Africa I have seen preachers in the dirtiest places sporting preacher-outfits similar to what is seen on Gospel television in a nice and tidy studio. I have seen mini-seminars and conferences held in metal shacks, and youth programs in slums that strive to be 'relevant'. Many were more than a bit confused when they saw that churches in America were beginning to allow homosexuals into leadership, and some posed the question, "Are we to allow this too?"

It may be strange that the world could be having a love-hate relationship with America. It definitely looks that way. It's rare to find a foreigner who wouldn't want to visit it, but it's not always easy to find a foreigner who loves it.

In the light of all this there is much we need to think about, pray over, and learn, whether you are a citizen from this "great city" or not. Our attitudes will affect how we respond to such significant things in the world and all attitudes must be brought and tested under the Word of God. There is great benefit to keeping oneself from being entangled with the affairs of this world. It behooves us therefore to take care with our attitudes towards America as it seems to be one of the greatest "entanglements" of our day—and perhaps of all time.

At the Head of Every Street

The orphan is verily vainly aware
of a woman lurking in a shadow of despair
Parched from thirst with nothing to eat
Stones lie scattered at the head of the street

Bereaved, alone, and a face black as soot
Lay he there hungry, trampled underfoot
Born on stony ground, in thickets unsweet
His mother scorns payment at the head of the street

Like an ostrich in the wild her cruelty goes
to cut off a child in the midst of her throes
No home, no name, no water, no meat
In anguish he lies at the head of the street

"Away! Unclean!" from their mouth they pour
"A wanderer, a fugative, the son of a whore!"
Pursued until dawn in bloody feet
From his mother's bosom at the head of the street

Is this the city? Of refuge and strength?
The perfection of beauty eternal at length?
The joy of the earth? A place so effete?
Lofty and high at the head of every street?

From Survival to Success

We tend to think that if Jesus Christ compels us to do something and we are obedient to Him, He will lead us to great success. We should never have the thought that our dreams of success are God's purpose for us. In fact, His purpose may be exactly the opposite. We have the idea that God is leading us toward a particular end or a desired goal, but He is not. The question of whether or not we arrive at a particular goal is of little importance, and reaching it becomes merely an episode along the way. What we see as only the process of reaching a particular end, God sees as the goal itself.

Oswald Chambers

THE CHURCH OF THE PAST

As society continues to break down and the Church around us seems to fall apart the thought comes to mind of the meaning of Success in our Postmodern Society. It seems as though Success has become the underlying motivation—or lure—for nearly everything we do. Our decisions that we make in life seem to revolve around Success. Whether we think we can have Success or think that Success has evaded us and we are incapable of finding it, our lives are reflecting more and more just how core that value is in our hearts as a Postmodern Society.

This hasn't always been the core value of humans however. The underlying mode of living has always been survival for human communities. Kingdoms, empires, nations, people groups, tribes, clans, and families have always been drawn together for the sake of survival. There was never really a question of being in an Dark World full of danger and evil. It was a world no one could survive on his own. God in the Old Testament held special compassion for the sojourner, the abandoned, the orphan, the widows, and the like because they were the ones who were alone and on their own. To be in such a state is not fitting for any human, because they will not last on their own—not in an evil, Dark World overtaken by spiritual wickedness, sin, and death.

The Church itself originally began as such a community. It was formed as a kingdom among kingdoms. It was a place meant to be a refuge and beacon of light to all the lost in the Dark World. The New Testament consistently and effectively emphasized the need for its members to work together, to love one another, and to support one another. It was a community of sojourners and pilgrims bonding together as one family that they might be strong and mighty in the midst of a Dark World. It was taught to do good to all, but especially to those of the Household of Faith. People came to seek salvation, healing, and protection because it was the only hope of survival for the meek, the lowly, the oppressed, and the downtrodden. It exuded a strength that could not ever be defeated though many of the Dark World tried to overcome it. Jesus had told that this was how it would be. He never promised the gates of hell would not touch it. He simply promised that they would never prevail against it. As a new and scattered community in the Dark World it was easy to bind together and strengthen one another to form a family that could resist and overcome the Dark World. And to help the Church out, God sent his greatest Gift to make it possible. The Church was a place of survival.

THE LURE OF GREATNESS

Going back to the beginning of the Holy Book we see a reminder of our worst enemy: our pride. It was how our first parents became slaves to the Dark World themselves. The tactic was clear and simple. Lure them with greatness, and the prospect of being glorious, like God even. What's wrong with wanting to be great after all? What's wrong with wanting to feel the glories of Success? Surely it is harmless. Go ahead, try it. You'll like it. You'll feel good. You deserve to feel good. Why, can't you see? You'll be letting others and God down if you don't make the most of Yourself and reach your highest potential. You are supposed to be successful and awesome like God. You were after all created in His Image, weren't you? And so has the disease plagued us ever since. All of us. Mankind has consistently been lured by Success.

Yet, for the most part, Success didn't find a place to call home in too many communities or kingdoms of the world. The Dark World was a difficult place to live for everyone. In fact, it was the lure of Success that destroyed it and made it difficult to live in in the first place. Technology, medicine, education, and wealth hardly existed, except for a very few elite persons. War was always immanent. Kingdoms subduing kingdoms and land being taken and retaken. The way of life was a way of survival and the tribe, clan, family, and kingdom communities were the only hope. It was never a sure hope, but it was, for most of humankind, the only hope. And so the drive was to fortify the family, the clan, or the tribe, and to strengthen and support your kingdom because, even if there were things you didn't like about it, it protected you as you sought to live in a Dark World. Protection and security was highly valued. Like any nuclear family, you would never split because of differences in interests or disagreements. You needed each other for the sake of survival as individuals in a Dark World. So Success had few occasions to do much damage on a wide scale.

POSTMODERN SOCIETY

With the arrival of a new kind of society in just the last hundred years everything changed. We began to believe our worst as humans. Somehow the Dark World became the Good World. We began to believe that we had the power to change it so. We discovered Technology, Medicine, Education, and Opportunity. We were led to believe that with these we could solve the problems of the world. It wasn't a Dark World anyway—it was a Good World that just needs some fixing. No longer did we have to worry about survival. It was time to think about Success. Much of the world however remains in survival mode, yet for the Postmodern Society this is not a problem. With a little bit of work and a little bit of time they will be enlightened themselves and they will understand.

The Postmodern Society then has brought an entirely new era to humankind–the way of life being built on the promise of Success and Greatness. There is no need for survival because all things and people are good. Tabula rasa. There is no evil here. Evil is something that can't be corrected without God. So if you take evil out of the equation all that really remains is a lack of Technology, Medicine, Education, and Opportunity—and humans can fix these. We don't need God. Subsequently, the opportunity for all of us as individuals to be great has far exceeded the opportunity to humans in any other age. Meaning and significance in family, tribe, clan, or kingdom became outdated and obsolete. They are unnecessary for Success and Greatness and in fact are liable to hold you back from it. The Postmodern Society speaks to its children with a lure so powerful and a promise so great that Adam and Eve themselves would probably turn over in their graves if they saw it. It tells its children that not only is it possible for you as an individual to be Great, but it is your *destiny* to be Great. Hope was quickly dislodged from being firmly established in a family and was transplanted in self: *I am the means to my own salvation, survival, and success.* The first act of disobedience by our parents finally found a place for total proliferation but this time forget about taking a single apple from the tree and eating it—we're gonna grow a whole damn orchard of apple trees, harvest them, and sell them for profit!

In addition, the daughters of Eve were to find themselves in a position that none of their mothers ever experienced. Women everywhere have found the lure afforded to them just as much as to the men of the Postmodern Society. They could make their own way to Greatness and Success. No longer did women need men or men need women for survival. There was no Dark World and there was no need for survival. Brothers didn't need each other. Sisters didn't need each other. In the Postmodern Society, Success is the name of the game and those things tend to get in the way anyway. There may be perhaps occasion to need them, but only so long as it is expedient to the Success of the individual and not survival. The question is no longer "Will they protect me?" but rather, "Will they make me Great and Successful?" So women and men leave each other in droves lured and enticed away by the illusion of Success. Child bearing turned into a commodity to be bought only if you felt it made you Greater. It also turned into a commodity to throw in the trash if it infringed on your Success. Sex was also made a commodity to find pacification in the Dark World and turned it into a meritorious achievement to earn status among men. You were not as successful and great as those who had more of it than you.

THE BREAKDOWN

Suffice it to say, a reality has begun to emerge that is showing our repeated, fatal flaw of eating the Apple. More people here live alone than at any other time in history. Countless children have been killed, aborted, destroyed, and orphaned in the name of Success. We didn't realize what all the divorce would really do to children. We figured for some time they would be fine. After all, you didn't need the family for survival anyway. We didn't realize that sex apart from marriage would leave us feeling trashed, empty, diseased with many physical illnesses, and left with the very thing that we considered a hindrance to our Success and Greatness (and in fact now makes even survival extremely difficult): fatherless and motherless children. We didn't realize these same children would end up committing mass murders in their schools, homicides on the streets, and suicides in their lonely houses—before they ever even grew up.

The Church, in its strong tendency to prostitute itself with the world—yes even the Dark World—was definitely not immune to the lure of Success and has become itself a means to Success and Greatness for many. More churches have died and are dying than we probably realize because of this. Some die because they are not great or Successful causing people to abandon them and leave them for dead in pursuit of Greatness.

very good

Other churches die because we try to build them and make them in the name of Greatness and Success and we know that such churches can never last very long before we find ourselves disillusioned with what we thought was going to be…Great. Or we find ourselves numbed to the reality of the Dark World, entranced by the feeling of Success, and losing sight of the light of the Word of God which tells us we are sojourners and pilgrims in a Dark World.

THE HOPE

God had destined a Family for his own possession—a Family of Hope and Salvation through the blood of his own dear family member—his Son. We as his people have lost sight of the purpose of his Church, the purpose of the family, and consequently our strength as a community to withstand the gates of hell. Being and meeting together as a Church, doing Church, and leading Church should never be a means to Greatness or Success. It was intended to be a refuge in the darkness and a place where we could not only survive, but thrive in the Dark World (a.k.a. survival abundantly). He who is in us is greater than he who is in the world. If we have the right objectives in mind, we are a light that the darkness cannot comprehend. But as long as we give ourselves to the lure of Success, our churches and our children will suffer. We must learn to come together to find strength and healing, not to find Greatness. Church is not a commodity or anyone's accomplishment. It will not work to lead Church, plant churches, start ministries, or open organizations with the idea of achievement and Success in mind just as we cannot lead and build families with the idea of success in mind. It simply does not work—it never has, and only leaves things in ruin. We have to come back to the reality that the Way of Life is about endurance and perseverance, and not accomplishment or Success. Endurance and perseverance is only possible with each other—we cannot make it alone. The sin of this lure is great, and we are all giving into it.

Israel, America, and the Church

Blessed is the nation whose God is the LORD, the people whom he has chosen as his heritage! Psalm 33:12

For thousands of years it was Israel and Israel alone that sought to walk according to God's ways as a nation (though often straying). Because of this the nation was continually blessed and protected. In this, they stood completely apart from any other nation. That is, until the 17th and 18th centuries. Almost suddenly, a new nation was born based on the ways of the God of Jerusalem: they called it America.[1]

Of course the wheat was not without its tares, and so there were antinomianists, legalists, bigots, racists, murderers, slave-traders, etc. Indeed, there was the ever-present human stench that follows wherever humans go. The heart of man, whether Christian or not, isn't tabula rasa like some would like to imagine. Sin goes where man goes. If America was ever a Christian nation, then it was a nation of repentant sinners under the grace of God, even of those repentant of legalism, racism, slave-trading, prostitution, etc. But the matter here isn't so much about whether it was "Christian" or not "Christian" but about the Word of the God of Israel. Regardless of how things went, the

---

[1] For uniqueness of Israel among nations see Exodus 3:15, 2 Chronicles, 32:19, etc.

Word of the God of Israel was there in the roots of this new nation.

Christian Puritans had come across the Atlantic to this new land to pursue freedom from persecution and start a "city on a hill" based on New Testament church models. Meanwhile, other groups had journeyed across seeking to exploit and pursue selfishness (the killing of Native Americans, bringing the slave trade, etc). But the thrust and the core of the new country was a community founded on the precepts of the God of Israel.

This is an astonishing piece of history because no other community, city, country, or kingdom that we know of has ever been founded and birthed on principles from the Word of God. In other countries there may have been religious transformations, adaptations, and reformations of various types, but not many nations can boast of being founded on a faith or religion. In this America stands apart from any other nation that ever existed except one: Israel. Israel was and is the only other nation that has ever been founded on the written Word of God. This gives Israel and America a very unique relationship in the world. It is overwhelmingly clear that God has immensely blessed America, and likewise Israel since it was reestablished. God prospers and blesses his people who walk according to his ways. [2]

It is for this reason, I believe, that the relationship between Israel and America has been like very close sisters. Perhaps more accurately as a mother-daughter-like relationship because "to them were given the oracles of God" and what we built owes itself

---

[2] Deuteronomy 28:9-14, 1 Kings 11:38, Psalm 119:2-3

to those oracles. America would not be what it has been if it were not for the nation of Israel, the keepers of the oracles of God.[3]

THE NEW DANGER

The growing pandemic of consumerism taking over the American church has put her into serious danger because she is putting trust in her wealth and beauty and openly fornicating in countless ways within the Christian context. It not only compromises but sells out the faith and openly throws away what is precious and sacred to wicked and desolate hands. She is forgetting her God and turning to wretchedness in the alleys and dark places looking for anything to feed her self-centeredness. Hence, she is taken advantage of, used, beaten up, and left wallowing in her blood. And those who pass by mock at her downfall.

The word on the streets today is as it has always been, "America is a Christian nation." No, not America's streets but the world's streets. The world knew and recognized this nation from its inception as a Christian nation. Only recently did that label begin to take a long painful plummet within America's own borders. American Church leaders today will not think twice about saying, "America is not a Christian nation." Nor will the majority of the population. The world understands however, that every single President of the United States has come from some Protestant Christian background (with exception to Kennedy who was Catholic) and has toted around and sworn themselves into office with a Bible—not a Qu'ran, nor a Tao-Te-Ching, nor

---

[3] Romans 3:2

a Sutra, nor a Bhagvad Gita, nor a Kojiki or Kujiki, nor a Veda. When foreigners bring their money to the exchange booths what do they see on printed all across our bills? "In God We Trust"

Christianity and Forms

This is very like the way to heaven; 'tis uphill. The Lord by His grace fetch us up. -John Eliot

It has been said that Christianity is "syncretistic at heart", and indeed, following the rise of Christianity from its beginnings through the Middle Ages, through the Reformation, into the early Puritanism of colonial America (not to mention the countless other nations and people groups around the world) and finally into the American Church of today one can clearly see that the Christian faith has a capacity for inheriting many different forms, customs, and expressions largely based on the contexts of culture, traditions, customs, and language. The important aspect of this however, lies in how Christianity is syncretistic—not in the case of belief system—but in the case of inflectional form. This is often referred to as *contextualization* or *incarnationalism*.

The teachings of Jesus were consistently centered on a fully otherworldly faith and belief system—a unique aspect among other major religions. The premise was a freedom from all religious law which in turn produced a faith that was to be unbound by any human standardization.

The very freedom of this unbound faith left the door wide open for interpretation into human standards and representations by countless leaders, rulers, and teachers, including Jesus himself. Consequently, the Christian faith has been able to present itself as a highly organic, workable, and formidable "religion". It is like play dough which, although always remaining of the same substance, may be shaped in an infinite number of ways.

Syncretism in Christianity may be interpreted in two ways. First is the syncretism of the *faith* with other *faiths*. This kind of syncretism would essentially yield an inter-religious faith which may not be as common a phenomenon as the second kind of syncretism—contextualization—which is between the Christian *faith* and *culture*. That is, a non-human and otherworldly belief system is coupled or bound within the constraints of human and worldly contexts, whether for good or for ill. This unique characteristic of the Christian faith has significantly contributed to its spread and is where we see the most formidable stance and progression of Christianity throughout all time. The sheer adaptability and "contextualizability" has allowed the otherworldly teachings of Jesus to take on forms of a gathering in a Jewish temple, to monks living in monastery, to a convent for set-apart religious women, to an entire political regime of a world empire, to a tribal gathering of Pacific Islanders, to a hippie commune for Jesus, to a hard-core band screaming for Jesus. It seems to know no limits.

The Original Form

In its beginnings, the teachings of Jesus were brought within the existing frameworks of the Jewish culture into which he was born. It was found among fishermen, tradesmen, and people who worked for the government,[1] and made use of their homes and dinner tables for worship meetings. Nothing was added, removed, or changed within the cultural norms. From such grassroot beginnings it spread infectiously rather than forcefully. "The

---

[1] Matthew 10:3, Luke 5:27

private domestic house served as the foundation for missional outreach and community formation in the primitive church in Jerusalem, just as it did in the ministry of Jesus and his disciples"[2]

The testimony of Jesus itself shows us an *incarnational* God who, though not a Jew, became a Jew and spoke in the Hebrew language. Through contextualization, God took on the form of a man and servant, even though he is neither.[3]

Other elements of the Jewish and Roman culture are observed. We see Jesus' formal entrance into Jerusalem which was a custom to signify the coming of a King and to which all the people responded accordingly by waving palm tree branches and crying, "Hosanna, Hosanna!"[4] We see Jesus teaching parables in the context of first century economic situations using vineyards, wineskins, winepresses, sheep, goats, farming, etc. for illustration. We also see Jesus teaching in the Jewish temple and their synagogues, and following a host of other Jewish customs.

The early Church followed Jesus in this manner as it took root through incarnating the gospel wherever it spread. Paul's own ambition was to make himself all things to all men in order to save more people.[5] It was not a matter compromising the gospel and making it less offensive, but rather following the pattern of Jesus by drawing as near to the common man as possible. Dean Flemming observes,

> Paul's ministry in Athens is a model of cultural sensitivity and adjustment to his audience. Paul demonstrates an awareness of

---

[2] Gehring, Roger W. *House Church and Mission: The Importance of Household Structures in Early Christianity*, (Hendrickson Publishers, Inc., 2004), 116-117.
[3] Numbers 23:19, Philippians 2:6-8
[4] John 12:13
[5] 1 Corinthians 9:19-23

Athenian culture that gains credibility and earns him the right to be heard. He keenly observes their religious beliefs and shows familiarity with their ancient literary and philosophical traditions. He uses this insight to respectfully engage their worldview, drawing upon indigenous language, images and concepts to communicate the gospel in culturally relevant forms…At the same time, Paul refuses to syncretize his message or to compromise its truth claims; we must do likewise.[6]

This pattern of spreading the gospel made the gospel and the Church so accessible that Christianity was able to spread like wild fire. People great and small alike discovered a faith which allowed them to worship God in any style, form, and place they wished. All were welcome to the table no matter what their background was as the God of this faith was impartial and forgave all.[7] For many religious leaders and rulers who loved their power and positions of control, this was a very threatening movement indeed.

THE MEDIEVAL FORM

Soon the faith would encompass so many people that the Roman Empire itself couldn't help but recant its official position of paganism to adopt an official position of Christianity.

In the early stages of Christianity as a minority faith within the Roman Empire, the Christians had to make do with the little freedom that they had. Even when the faith was tightly

---

[6] Dean E. Flemming, *Contextualization in the New Testament: Patterns for Theology and Mission.* (Downers Grove, IL: InterVarsity Press, 2005). p.82
[7] Romans 2:11, Mark 3:28

constrained and oppressed under emperors such as Nero and Diocletian, it still flourished since it was already well accustomed to homes and private spheres of life. Christian assemblies were made up of both men and women. Unlike trade associations and cultic brotherhoods which were gender specific, the burgeoning church manifested its value of equality without compromise. The faith was equally for all and to all.[8] Neither were the poor and destitute excluded but, in fact, were a central part of the Christian communities' activity. Afflicted and needy believers "grew like thick layers of bark around every Christian community…The destitute alone were more numerous than the entire membership of all but the largest professional association in the city."[9]

Soon the persecutions would subside, having failed to achieve what they intended, and the empire would embrace the Christian faith. In 313, the emperor Constantine declared, "we should therefore give both to Christians and to all others free facility to follow the religion which each may desire…"[10] His hope was to secure favor and benevolence from the "Supreme Godhead". From here politics began to take hold of the Christian faith and carry it on in its own way to the nations of the world. As paganism dilapidated and the Christian faith strengthened the old Latin word *religio* which referred to a diverse culture of traditional pagan rites called *religiones*, was now used to refer to the Roman empire's new official *religio*: the worship of Christ.[11] The transitions seemed easier to deal with when established customs

---

[8] Brown, Peter. *The Rise of Western Christendom: Triumph and Diversity, A.D. 200-1000*. Second Edition. (Blackwell Publishing Ltd., 2003), p.64
[9] Ibid. p.70
[10] Constantine's *Edict of Milan*. A.D. 313
[11] Brown, Peter. p.74

and socio-lingual concepts could be used with a new belief system.

By the fifth century, the idea of saints, monks, popes, and Christian aristocracy had entered the newly established Christian cultural scene. Asceticism and the monastic life became a popular movement. Such figures as St. Antony became famed as a monk who, upon hearing the verse read out of Matthew 19:21 in church one day, went and sold everything he had and lived without material possessions, without home, without family, always giving away his food, and working only with his hands. "Conducting himself in this way, then, Antony was loved by everyone."[12]

The concept of "pope" began to take root as more and more bishops of various churches and regions began to capitulate towards the bishop of Rome who was called a *papa,* the commonplace word for "father" in Greek, Latin, and Italian. It was a common title used for any senior bishop. The bishop of Rome however had come to play an "elder role" for other less-experienced regions burgeoning with the Christian faith, and eventually Rome became established as the seat of St. Peter upon which Catholics believe the church is founded.[13] At the same time, the Christian faith found its way into the aristocratic way of life. In France particularly, experimentations with church leadership and government lead to what ultimately was the most enduring form: the "aristocratization" of church. "In the fifth century, the landed aristocracy of Gaul…took over the government of the Church…As a result…Gaul became very

---

[12] Athanasius of Alexandria, *Life of St. Antony of Egypt,* trans. David Brakke, in *Medieval Hagiography: An Anthology,* ed. Thomas Head (New York: Garland, 2000), pp. 7-29

[13] Brown, Peter. *The Rise of Western Christendom,* p.114

different from Italy, North Africa, and the eastern empire, whose clergy tended to represent, rather, the middling classes of the cities."[14]

Reform was a typical characteristic of Christianity over time. It is interesting to note how the various expressions of the faith put forth by different leaders often led to either a progression or regression of the faith. St. Augustine in the fifth century fueled a reform of the Christian world as a feeling of disillusionment pervaded the continent after Alaric's sack of Rome in 410. Pagans took up the opportunity to criticize Christianity as Rome was a Christian empire that fell apart.[15] St. Augustine however, upheld and emphasized the Christian faith as an otherworldly 'city' subject to God's discourse, and not a city of this world subject to man's discourse.

By the eighth century the Christian faith found itself undergoing new continental reform. A man known as Boniface undertook missionary work among the pagan Saxons east of the Rhine River. The region was Christianized, but had suffered from inter-religious syncretism and serious regression into former pagan ways. "Cultic practitioners exchanged rituals [with Christians]. Pagans baptized Christians. Christian priests sacrificed to Thunor…"[16] Boniface had a radical attitude towards reaching the people in this part of the world in contrast to the present ruler of the time, King Charles, also known as Charlemagne. Charlemagne wished to enforce conversion of the Saxon pagans to Christianity by law, subjecting them to imprisonment or death if they would not be baptized[17]. His

---

[14] Ibid. p.110
[15] Ibid. p.91
[16] Ibid. p.420
[17] King Charlemagne, *Capitulary concerning the Parts of Saxony (785)*

method of inflecting the faith was apparently through political and military force. Boniface however, preferred to meet the Saxons on their own terms—to contextualize—and even went so far as to change his name to follow the Saxon custom of taking on a Roman name. Hence, he permanently changed his name from Wynfrith to Boniface.[18] "He declared, *"the customs of past ages"* must be measured by *"the correct taste of modern times."* For him the classical past was irrelevant…He stood for a new form of Christianity, unburdened by the past."[19] He wanted to progress the Christian faith inflectionally. On the other hand, King Charlemagne wanted to regress to the ways of the Old Testament tradition. In his *Admonitio Generalis* written in 789, he declared,

> …according to what the Lord ordained in the law, that there be no servile work on Sundays…that men do no farm work…nor are they to gather for games or go hunting. Three tasks with wagons may be performed on Sunday, the arms' cart or the food wagon, or if it is necessary to bear someone's body to the grave. Likewise, women are not to work with cloth nor cut out clothes…or shear sheep, to the end that the honor and quiet of the Lord's day be kept.[20]

An important factor of Charlemagne's version of Christianity was the role it played in the influence of culture. Outside of Charlemagne's empire in the various provinces of Europe, "culture tended to drain upward to the capital, to gather around the court and the offices of the patriarchate." Within Charlemagne's empire however, "the court acted as a 'distribution

---

[18] Brown, Peter, *The Rise of Western Christendom*, p.419
[19] Ibid. pp.418-419
[20] King Charlemagne, *The Admonitio Generalis* (789). Chapter 81.

center' both for books and for personnel." Educators, administrators, and clergy were pooled in and then sent out to various monasteries and churches.[21]

One of the most impressive examples of a contextual expression of the Christian faith in the medieval era may have had to do with the Iconoclast controversy. Art was already a large part of the Roman culture and involved the use of frescos, base and capital architecture, reliefs, mosaics, and sculpture. It was inevitable then that the Christian faith should find its way into some form of Roman art—and it did. All the characteristics of Roman art manifested themselves in Christendom. Iconophiles were known for expressing and reverencing the Christian faith through images and art, including mosaics, sculpture, reliefs, and frescos. This expression was soon challenged by those known as Iconoclasts—mainly Byzantine clergy and some bishops from Spain—who argued that these expressions were merely forms of idolatry, rather than contextualizations. Since freedom of the religion swept the empire in the fourth century, images and art pervaded the Christian church. But once again the cultural "inflection" of the Christian faith became a heated issue. "The Byzantine clergy were as intensely concerned...that 'orthodox' belief should be reflected in uniform traditions of worship observed throughout the empire."[22] One man, by the name of John of Damascus, stood up for the cause of images. In successfully arguing for the use of images, John shows very clearly the essence of the Christian faith as an inflectional, mobile religion:

---

[21] Brown, Peter. p.443
[22] Ibid. p.387

Images are a source of profit, help and salvation for us since they make hidden things clearly manifest to us, enabling us to perceive realities otherwise hidden to human eyes…In God, too, there are representations and images of His future acts— that is to say, His counsel from all eternity, which is ever unchangeable…Again, visible things are images of invisible and intangible things, on which they throw a faint light. Holy Scripture clothes in figure God and the angels…When sensible things sufficiently render what is beyond sense, and give a form to what is intangible, a medium would be reckoned imperfect according to our standard, if it did not fully represent material vision, or if it required effort of mind. If, therefore, Holy Scripture, providing for our need, ever putting before us what is intangible, clothes it in flesh, does it not make an image of what is thus invested with our nature, and brought to the level of our desires, yet invisible?[23]

Creativity then, on account of figures like John of Damascus, continued forth strongly as a "tradition" of the Christian faith.

The Christian faith has long proved itself to be a highly versatile and mobile "religion" just as easily subject to creative expression and inflection as it was to rock-hard traditions. While much of Christendom sought to form and reform in a spirit of progress, and to be a universally accessible faith as Augustine advocated[24], there always remained the need for a stable, conservative, and foundational core of what the Christian faith represented. "Rome gave the much-needed dimension of antiquity to "micro-Christendoms" which saw themselves, for all their immense creativity, as in need of a past."[25]

---

[23] John of Damascus, *On Holy Images*, c.730

[24] Augustine, *City of God*, (413-426)

[25] Brown, Peter. *The Rise of Western Christendom*, p.430

THE POST-REFORMATION FORM

Protestant Christianity took a big detour from much of the antiquity at this point, keeping only what it found to be fundamental to the faith. Pastors were elevated to the heads of the local church and the priesthood was scratched. The traditional vestments for the liturgy of the Catholic church were replaced by a Geneva gown—a black robe which served to hide fashion and grooming habits and to signify the office of a preacher. In effect, the robe hid anything that would otherwise be relevant to the culture of the day. The printing press was harnessed and the common man was for the first time able to own his own bible and study it for himself. The beginning of the 17th century saw the popularizing of organ music and many famous hymns. Charles and John Wesley founded the Methodist movement through the contextualization of preaching, music, and social organization which resulted in wide-spread revival in the eighteenth century. This time also gave birth to the Seminary, a result of Catholic reforms which has since become the educational standard for clergy and ministers seeking to enter ministry as a vocation.

THE PURITAN FORM

American Christianity itself started out as a micro-Christendom. The new frontier of America was inhabited by groups of Puritans who planted the first seeds of what was to become the world's most powerful national Church: the

American Church. The puritan form was based on European and Post-reformation methodology and practice. In essence, it was a transplant of the existing Puritan church in England carrying with it all the methodologies, practices, and traditions, as well as developing a few new ones. There was some ambition to reach the unreached tribal peoples of the new land, but this was overshadowed by the more prevalent theme of establishing a pure form of Christianity for an example to the rest of the world. Figures like John Winthrop proclaimed to followers that they would form a new society that would be "as a city upon a hill".[26] The new Church at large did not give itself to the cause of the natives. Figures like John Eliot and David Brainerd were among the few who made many sacrifices to reach the unreached tribes as well as to preserve their culture while teaching them the gospel.

The American version of Puritanism was distinct and definitely had its personal flavors to go with the times, the place, and the circumstances. However, it still carried with it much of the same legalistic and Gnostic tendencies of that which they had left in Europe. The separation between sacred and secular remained deeply rooted in the way of life for the new American Church. In their worldview the meeting-house, as it was called, was the sacred place for worship. It was labeled and called "the church" from then on, even though some were bitterly opposed to calling the edifice a church.[27] Sunday as well was called "the Sabbath" day. The design was a simple square building with a "truncated pyramidal roof which was surmounted...with a belfry or turret containing a bell."[28] These meeting houses became the

---

[26] Excerpted from Winthrop's sermon (pp. 63-65) in *Speeches That Changed the World*, compiled by Owen Collins. Westminster John Knox Press (1999).
[27] Alice Morse Earle, *The Sabbath in Puritan New England.* 1893 p.1
[28] Ibid. p.3

center-piece of the townships and were required in every new settlement. Colonists were required by law to build their new homes within half a mile of the meeting-house. Eventually meeting-houses were built on the hill-tops where it often served as a watch-house to keep a lookout against Indians. In the town the meeting-houses often would serve as a town-hall and storehouse, and sometimes—mischievously—as a place to store and sell tobacco. Wolves presented a major difficulty for the new American Church and many of the earliest meeting-houses would bear "grinning wolves' heads nailed under the windows and by the side of the door, while splashes of blood, which had dripped from the severed neck, reddened the logs beneath." In one town any man who brought a living wolf to church was paid fifteen shillings by the town, and if it was dead, ten shillings. To obtain the reward the hunter had to bring it and nail it to the meeting-house.[29]

In the front yards of the meeting-house stood "those Puritanical instruments of punishment, the stocks, whipping post, pillory, and cage." The stocks and pillory were often occupied by the Quakers, who also presented a "difficulty" to the new church, for they were often interrupting services and prophesying against the legalism and hypocrisy. In fact, there were fines for missing church attendance. The Quakers were poorly treated by the early American churches. Writes Earle, "…the Quakers contributed liberally to the support of the Court, and were fined in great numbers for refusing to attend the church which they hated, and which also warmly abhorred them; and they were zealously set in the stocks, and whipped and caged and pilloried as well—whipped if they came and expressed

---

[29] Ibid. p.11

dissatisfaction, and whipped if they stayed away."[30] The sermon was still the center of the public worship service, after the post-reformation fashion. The Puritans took pride in the centrality of the preaching and built pulpits more grand than the meeting-house itself. While the building was little more than an unpainted pine-smelling wooden shack with clear windows and hard bench seats the pulpit was typically a high desk to which a flight of stairs led, decorated and ornamented with pillars and panels. Some had a small door into which the minister walked "while the children counted the seconds from the time he closed the door until his head appeared through the trap-door at the top." One pulpit was known to have "as its sole decoration, an enormous, carefully painted, staring eye, a terrible and suggestive illustration to youthful wrong-doers of the great, all-seeing eye of God."[31]

Because Indians were also seen as a threat to the public assemblies there were laws requiring men to bring their loaded weapons along to church, and a "Sabbath-Day guard" was established. Entire plans for emergencies were created for protecting and evacuating women and children. Men were to sit at the "head" of the pews ready to seize their arms and rush to a fight. They would be the first to rise and leave the meeting-house so as to make a sure and safe exit for the women and children.[32]

The idea of the "tithingman" arose in 1668 to manage disorderly youths and would "use such raps and blows as in his discretion meet." The tithingman was known to be the "most grotesque, the most extraordinary, the most highly colored figure in the dull New England church-life" and carried with him a staff

---

30 Ibid. p.251
31 Ibid. p.16
32 Ibid. p.24

equipped with a hard knob at one end and a fox tail at the other. This was used to whop laughing youths and snoozing men and tickle awake the faces of sleeping ladies. They also carried authority throughout the week and not just on Sundays. They enforced the learning of the catechism at home, watched over the activities of youths, monitored peoples' drinking habits, spied on bachelors, and regulated riding and working on the Sabbath. They would often arrest people and have them put in the stocks and cages along with the sleepers from church.[33]

Eventually the Church started to get a little more creative and, as usual, it was always met with opposition. There was a move to paint the meeting-houses some interesting colors and to add cushions to the benches. When a Colonel in Newbury town cushioned his pew at the turn of the 18th century there was "a nine days' talk" among the people over it.[34] When a new meeting-house in Pomfret, Connecticut was painted bright yellow, "it proved to be a veritable golden apple of discord throughout the county."[35] The idea of the Sunday school emerged at the turn of the 19th century and was originally called "Sabbath school". It was not well received either. The Salem Gazette newspaper at first condemned the idea as profaning the Sabbath and such schools were banned from many churches for years.[36] The music was strictly controlled and there was no little dispute over it. Some clergy insisted on a universal form using the "Bay Psalm-Book, perhaps not being far from the same spirit of the Byzantines centuries earlier in wanting to enforce a uniform

---

[33] Ibid. p.66-76
[34] Ibid. p.43
[35] Ibid. p.15
[36] Ibid. p.108

tradition of worship. Earle writes,

> So villainous had church-singing at last become that the clergymen arose in a body and demanded better performances; while a desperate and disgusted party was also formed which was opposed to all singing. Still another band of old fogies was strong in force who wished to cling to the same way of singing that they were accustomed to; and they gave many objections to the new-fangled idea of singing by note, the chief item on the list being the everlasting objection of all such old fossils, that "the old way was good enough for our fathers,". They also asserted that *"the names of the notes were blasphemous;"* that it was "popish;" that it was a contrivance to get money; that it would bring musical instruments into the churches...[37]

The opposition would not prevail for long however, and soon the American Church would once again be transformed with the coming of new generations and new creativities to produce the most powerful and dominant forms of the Christian Church to date.

THE AMERICAN FORM

Understanding the present form of the American Church is a complicated undertaking. Since the Puritan days, the American Church has exploded into 20,000 denominations, and not only denominations, but multitudes of parachurches, mission agencies, political parties, and other ministry organizations. In fact,

---

[37] Ibid. p.208

denominationalism is an American phenomenon. As immigrants poured in over the centuries, they brought with them their old state church practices and forms with them. Then the denominations splintered into more denominations.

Today, denominationalism is quickly becoming an old fad as nearly every major denomination is losing ground. Barry Kosmin, the co-author of the American Religious Identification Survey (ARIS) recently performed in 2008, states, "More than ever before, people are just making up their own stories of who they are. They say, 'I'm everything. I'm nothing. I believe in myself...'"[38] Mega-churches have been a recent phenomenon in the last few decades, seeing some of the most high-tech and expensive Christian forms in history. Most recently, the American Church has expanded into pubs, theaters, schools, under bridges, and throughout homes. At the same time America has become, for better or worse, an exporter of all these forms in its carrying the gospel to other parts of the world.

As more and more Africans were brought over for the slave trade, African forms began to emerge. During the time of slavery there was a wide-spread effort to "de-Africanize" the slaves which resulted in restrictions on their church gatherings against dancing, instruments, and "pagan" ways of shouting and stomping in circles. Sometimes benches were put in their gathering places to prevent them from jumping up and dancing. Of course, the African style could not be snuffed out and freed Africans eventually banded together to start a movement of their own form of the faith rooted in African spirituals, instruments, jazz

---

[38] Grossman, Cathy. "Most religious groups in USA have lost ground, survey finds." *USA Today* 17 Mar. 2009. Accessed 23 Aug. 2009 <http://www.usatoday.com/news/religion/ 2009-03-09-american-religion-aris_n.htm>.

and blues innovations, and dancing. Gospel music began by the late 19ᵗʰ century and eventually led into the urban gospel music of today.

As a result there is a great rift between the Church of the white population and the Church of the black population that persists today. The Native American population, after being forced to "Westernize" over the centuries, has only recently begun to recapture its heritages and ancient cultures within the context of the gospel.

Now, heading into the 21ˢᵗ century, the American Church is undergoing yet another major shift and "reformation" as the old form consisting of the hymnal, pews, organ, dressy attire, choirs, and hierarchy is dying out everywhere and giving way to youthful, zealous, and informal community gatherings utilizing a wide variety of music styles, artistic expressions, and locations for congregating. The word on the streets is "out of the box" Christianity.

***

John of Damascus writes of Gregory asserting that "the mind which is set upon getting beyond corporeal things, is incapable of doing it."[39] John Drane, a professor of practical theology at the University of Aberdeen writes, "Worship, of all aspects of church life, ought to create a context in which people can be themselves, which is another way of saying that we need spaces where we may celebrate the way God has made us. By definition, that means there will never be any universalized blueprint for relevant

---

[39] John of Damascus, *On Holy Images*, c.730

worship…"[40] Clearly the Gospel is intended to be spread through contextualization through the things we can see, hear, and feel. Change in our forms is inevitable, not because Christ or the Gospel changes, but because the world and its people change. It must be done with discernment and good judgment as well. Dean Flemming exhorts us,

> Like Paul, we must critique our own culture without rejecting it, and transcend our culture even while remaining in it. Likewise, we must be willing to identify with another's culture without uncritically accommodating to it; we must let the gospel speak transformingly to that culture without imposing a foreign culture upon it. This is the calling of the missional church in every place and every generation.[41]

The most effective work of spreading the Gospel will have in mind Romans 1:20 which says that the invisible things of God are made visible through images. It is what Andrew Walls describes as the gospel being imprisoned and liberating at the same time. He writes,

> Along with the indigenizing principle which makes his faith a place to feel at home, the Christian inherits the pilgrim principle, which whispers to him that he has no abiding city and warns him that to be faithful to Christ will put him out of step with his society; for that society never existed, in East or West, ancient time or modern, which could absorb the word of Christ painlessly into its system. Jesus within Jewish culture,

---

[40] Drane, John. *The McDonaldization of the Church: Consumer Culture and the Church's Future.* Macon, GA: Smyth &Helwys Publishing, Inc., 2001. p.197
[41] Dean E. Flemming, *Contextualization in the New Testament: Patterns for Theology and Mission.* (Downers Grove, IL: InterVarsity Press, 2005). p.151

Paul within Hellenistic culture, take it for granted that there will be rubs and friction—not from the adoption of a new culture, but from the transformation of the mind towards that of Christ.[42]

This very aspect may be a reason why, ultimately, the Christian faith cannot be manifestly known in and of itself—for it is eternal and invisible—but known only through form and ritual in which there is a relative freedom of expression.

The call of the Church therefore is to gain believers by all means, in whatever form, custom, language, culture, or artistic expression may be necessary so long as it does not compromise its message of truth. It is *through* diversity that we must seek unity, not around it.

Jesus said to her, "Woman, believe me, the hour is coming when neither on this mountain nor in Jerusalem will you worship the Father…God is spirit, and those who worship him must worship in spirit and truth. John 4:21,24

---

[42] Andrew Walls, "The Gospel as the Prisoner and Liberator of Culture," *Missionalia* 10, no. 3 (November 1982): 98-99.

Culture of the Fatherless

The Lord is a man of war; the Lord is his name. Exodus 15:3

O men, how long shall my honor be turned into shame? How long will you love vain words and seek after lies? Selah. But know that the Lord has set apart the godly for himself; the Lord hears when I call to him. (Psalm 4:3)

For thus the LORD said to me, "As a lion or a young lion growls over his prey, and when a band of shepherds is called out against him he is not terrified by their shouting or daunted at their noise, so the LORD of hosts will come down to fight on Mount Zion and on its hill. Isaiah 31:4

The wicked flee when no one pursues, but the righteous are bold as a lion. Proverbs 28:1

Be watchful, stand firm in the faith, act like men, be strong. 1 Corinthians 16:13

In 1908 John R. Mott, the general secretary of the World's Student Christian Federation, proclaimed, "If the Church is to grow, so as to meet the growing needs of the age, it must have able men in its ministry…Without such leadership there is danger that it will ultimately be reduced to a negligible force."[1] A

---

[1] Mott, John R. *The Future Leadership of the Church.* New York: Young Men's Christian Association, 1909. p.4

hundred years later we are seeing Mott's prophetic proclamation coming true.

In our society, 70-80% of boys are growing up with a totally uninvolved, distant, or absent father.[2] 95% of boys learn to cut off all their emotions except anger by the age of nine.[3] What we are in effect left with is a society of boys in men's clothing. Because of the way materialism has deceived our culture by leading us to believe manhood can be bought, the design and purpose of masculinity has been profoundly compromised. The true art and design of manhood has been forgotten. What we have been told is that the measure of a true man is defined by his material gain and sexual prowess. Yet God in his infinite wisdom created the man to be a guardian and protector—not an exploiter. His purpose was to keep and take care of his home (Genesis 2:15). In the American culture however, the majority of men will continue to stare in the mirror in confusion about who they are throughout their lives. Of course, you might never have guessed this for these same men will live much of their lives as imposters, pretending to be men, or worse, convinced that they really are by what they have accumulated, accomplished, or what they have identified themselves with. They live in constant competition with their neighbor because, for them, manliness is measured by how much you can out-do other men. How big is *your* truck? How much can *you* bench press? How many ladies have *you* been with? How much have *you* accumulated? How much have *you* accomplished? Our culture is so deceived that *everyone* is found to believe these gross errors—mothers, fathers,

---

[2] Morman MT, Floyd K. A "Changing Culture of Fatherhood": effects on affectionate communication, closeness, and satisfaction in men's relationships with their fathers and sons. West J Speech Communications. 2002

[3] Michael Gurian, *Mothers, Sons & Lovers* (Shambhala Publications, 1994). 36

sons, and daughters alike. The feminist movements' decrying of patriarchy is not so much in reaction to God's design and purpose of masculinity as it is to their perceived understanding of it. They have witnessed the bitter testimony—often in personal way—of destructive and exploitative man-imposters, rather than the glory of protectors and guardians. They, along with the rest of our society, have forgotten what a true man is really about.

All the while an essential spiritual transition is left undone. Fathers are distant or gone, or have never understood properly their own identity as men, and so their sons are not initiated into God's design of manhood—as protectors and keepers of their homes. Instead, they learn to live in a fear of life and are content with merely trying to survive it. But they are never truly happy, because they are constantly overcome when they subject themselves, or find themselves subjected to life's various duties that require *men* and not boys. They also become unprotective and even destructive to their home environments, because they live in a fearful survival mode and not in a protector mode. This is perhaps what has made our society so environmentally unconscious and destructive. Proving our manhood, then, is no longer committing to the protection of the home front, but declaring "I'm not afraid of a damned thing", or feeling powerful through materialism and consumerism, or seeing how many women we can get into bed—the very things that marketers of popular culture cater to and feed off of. Indeed, our culture and society teach men to never leave adolescence. Adolescence is, in fact, more of a bondage than a transition in that it holds a would-be man in a confusing tension between boyhood and manhood. They are spiritually and emotionally void of manhood, though physically and mentally matured as men. Thus, in their relationships with women or wives they will long for the emotional support of their mother—whose safe attachment they have not separated from—and, at the same time, will push away from them because they must "be the man" through the false pretense of sexual conquest. A woman's deepest need in marriage is for *God's design of manhood.* That is how he created it to be. That design centers on the spiritual and emotional side of being a man. The highest duty of a husband, according to the Apostle Paul, is that he *love* his wife (Ephesians 5:25). Love is a spiritual and emotional element long before it is anything else. The opposite of love is fear. To live in a fear of life is to be entirely unloving; to live according to your duty as a protector is entirely loving and courageous. Yet the uninitiated boy-man knows nothing of how to use his emotions in a manful way as God intended but instead suppresses them or looks for nurturance of them from the woman like a second emotional mother—either the one he couldn't let go of or never had—and seeks other pretentious ways to prove himself to the woman.

So then, let us ask ourselves a serious question. If this is the case with the vast majority of men, then what can we say of what is happening with our Church? What can we possibly do if this deception is destroying our churches, our leaders, our marriages and relationships, and our society? To begin with, 40% of church-goers are male. Women are more likely to read the scriptures, pray, do missions, and attend church than men.[4] Author and Professor Leon J. Podles sheds some interesting light on the situation:

> Men can be taught to be men only by other men, and all too

---

[4] Leon J. Podles, *"Missing Fathers of the Church",* Touchstone January/February 2001

many pastors are not real men. A pastor called me about my book. He had been ordained in the mainline Presbyterian Church. When he entered the seminary, he had to take a battery of psychological tests and talk to a psychiatrist. The psychiatrist looked over the tests, and the first question he asked the candidate was, "Are you a homosexual?" The candidate responded, "No, I'm not, and why do you ask?" The psychiatrist replied, "You have the psychological profile of a homosexual. But don't worry, *all the successful ministers in your denomination have this profile.*"[5]

The prophetic vision of the Church is that of a Bride, Mother, and Whore. The Bible refers to her in this way because it is through her that we all receive the implanted word of truth. It is she who was commissioned to carry forth the blessing of Abraham to all nations, the seed of faith, the gospel of the Kingdom. She gives birth to many children around the world. She rears them as babes in Christ through discipleship using the milk of the Word, so that they might become men and women of God able to handle the meat of truth.[6] The Lord himself declares, *"Your maker is your husband."* (Isaiah 54:5) The Apostle Paul wrote, *"But the Jerusalem above is free, and she is our mother. For it is written, "Rejoice, O barren one who does not bear; break forth and cry aloud, you who are not in labor! For the children of the desolate one will be more than those of the one who has a husband."* (Galatians 4:26) St. Augustine is quoted as saying, "The Church is a whore, but she's my mother." Bishop Cyprian, declared in 251 A.D., "Thus also the Church, shone over with the light of the Lord, sheds forth her rays over the whole world, yet it is one

---

[5] Ibid.
[6] *See Isaiah 54:1-17; James 1:21; Galatians 3:14; Hebrews 5:11-14*

light which is everywhere diffused, nor is the unity of the body separated. Her fruitful abundance spreads her branches over the whole world. She broadly expands her rivers, liberally flowing, yet her head is one, her source one; and she is one mother, plentiful in the results of fruitfulness: from her womb we are born, by her milk we are nourished, by her spirit we are animated…He can no longer have God for his Father who has not the Church for his Mother."[7]

When you bring a generation of boy-men into a local church what you end up with is a heavy burden that the church cannot handle, nor is its leadership—if they are also void of real masculinity—able to handle. Such adolescent men seek for what they can get out of the church rather than how they can empower it, provide for it, and share with it. They exploit it rather than protect it. A real man of God will pour himself out; for when it comes to the Kingdom of God, he measures his life by loss instead of gain.[8] He serves and protects, provides and sustains. Meanwhile, the Church engages more and more in adulterous behavior as she compromises her dignity and gives in to worldly values. She is clueless about what to do with the fatherless as well as the widows and neglects to take care of them.[9]

---

[7] Bishop Cyprian, Treatise I. On the Unity of the Church. p423. 251 A.D.

[8] *"Measure your life by loss instead of gain. Not by the wine drunk, but by the wine poured forth. For love's strength standeth in love's sacrifice. And whosoever suffereth most hath most to give."* Ugo Bassi (1800-1849) From a sermon entitled "Love's Sacrifice".

[9] See James 1:27. The theme of caring for the fatherless and the widow is poignant throughout the scriptures: Exo 22:22-24; Deu 10:18; 14:28-29; 24:17-22; Deu 27:19; Job 22:9; 29:12-13; Psa 27:10; 68:5; 94:6; 146:9; Pro 23:10-11; Isa 1:17; 1:23; Isa 10:1-2; Jer 5:28; 7:6; 22:3; Jer 49:11; Hos 14:3; Mal 3:5

The answer to this dilemma is a fatherly redemption. And that redemption has a name: The Lord Jesus Christ. The one of whom Isaiah proclaimed, *"Everlasting Father".*[10] He is the truth that will free us from the deceptions. This one man alone will heal every wound left by mothers and fathers hindering boys from becoming men, redeem and restore every church from weak and failing masculinity, save every marriage from confused and overcome husbands and wives, and light up a selfish and materialistic society with living examples of what it means to be a *real man.* Christ was the ultimate man living the ultimate manhood by laying his righteous life down for the lives of sinners—the true protector and keeper of us all. May our fathers and mentors rise up and raise up *men*, and may our churches become supportive communities for them!

---

[10] Isaiah 9:6

Culture of Self

...the body does not consist of one member but of many.
1 Corinthians 12:14

The American worldview seems to have reached extremes with the glorification of self. Intellectuals are calling it *hyper-individualism* or *radical individualism*. Louis Dumont writes, "In the last decades, some of us have become increasingly aware that modern individualism, when seen against the background of the other great civilisations that the world has known, is an exceptional phenomenon."[1] This radical individualism is perhaps the greatest challenge to the American Church today. Instead of our churches preaching and living the message that a Kingdom of Heaven is at hand and that we must give up our former lives and join it, what we hear a lot of is a message of a personal kingdom just for *you*. Michael Horton notes, "Regardless of denomination, the American Religion is inward, deeply distrustful of institutions, mediated grace, the intellect, theology, creeds, and the demand to look outside of oneself for salvation."[2] It is by no means of recent development—even the famed Alexis de Tocqueville saw it pointedly 170 years ago:

---

[1] Dumont, Louis, "A modified view of our origins: the Christian beginnings of modern individualism." Carrithers, Michael, Steven Collins, and Steven Lukes, eds. *The Category of the Person*. New York, NY: Cambridge University Press, 1985.
[2] Horton, Michael S. "Gnostic Worship." *Modern Reformation* "Gnosticism" July/August Vol. 4 No. 4 (1995): 13-21.

To escape from imposed systems is their goal, and to seek by themselves and in themselves for the only reason for things, looking to results without getting entangled in the means toward them...So each man is narrowly shut up in himself, and from that basis makes the pretension to judge the world...Thus the Americans have needed no books to teach them philosophic method, having found it in themselves.[3]

Gnosticism is a belief system which emphasizes the *self* and that the inner self is where we will find "truth" and salvation. From this we also get the dualistic worldview of "sacred vs. secular". The good, or sacred, is the inner, intangible self and all matter is evil or secular. It is a theme that is widely argued to have pervaded the entire religious landscape of America as well as the American culture itself though it has been a part of the Western Church for many centuries.

The category of the sacred became limited to things that reflect the immaterial such as our "inner spiritual life" or the vocation of a missionary, priest, or pastor, while the secular or godless category was everything else. Brian Walsh suggests that "this dualism identifies obedience, redemption and the kingdom of God with only *one* area of life...It sees the rest of life as either unrelated to redemption (or the sacred), or worse—under the power of disobedience, sin and the kingdom of darkness."[4] A well known example of this dualistic-Gnostic way of thinking is the ongoing struggle in the Church with the music culture. Over time, the Church has categorized certain types of music into a "Christian" or sacred category, and other types which don't meet

---

[3] Alexis De Tocqueville. *Democracy in America.* trans. and ed. by J. P. Mayer and G. Lawrence. New York, NY: Harper and Row, 1988. p. 429.
[4] Brian J. Walsh, p.95.

the "Christian" criteria into a "secular" category. The lines between the two categories have always been vague, yet the dissensions and divisions it has caused within the Church have been anything but. Another example is Creation itself. Is it good or is it evil? Gnosticism says it is purely evil—including our own bodies—and we are seeking the liberation of our souls from it. St. Augustine thought this way as a Manichee, but later opposed it after his redemptive experiences. Scripture itself has only said this about creation: it is good, and God values it.[5] That's more than sufficient to teach us that it has a sacred value. Yet this Gnostic-dualism and our radical individualism have come together to create, literally, a culture of narcissism. H. Paul Santmire writes,

> Insofar as American Christianity has become the captive of radical individualism, which has been particularly attractive to Protestants, American Christianity may have become vulnerable to, if not totally made the captive of, the Gnostic spirit. Think of the "Me Culture," memorably called the "Culture of Narcissism" by Christopher Lasch, promulgated and sustained by mass advertising in our era: what really matters in this world is my peace of mind, my comfort, my security, my freedom to drive whatever I want to drive and to eat whatever I want to eat and to consume as many resources as I want to consume and to believe in a "god" that I want to believe in. Spiritually, likewise, what really matters is my own sin, my own conversion, and my own soul.[6]

---

[5] Genesis 1:31; Luke 12:24
[6] Santmire, H. P. *Ritualizing Nature*. Minneapolis, MN: Fortress Press, 2008. p.103.

The problem we face as followers of Christ is how to overcome this with *genuine belief* that we are collectively one temple of the Holy Spirit, called to uphold social justice and ecological justice *together* and not individually. Most of us understand this but have yet to believe it and live it out. Creation includes us and is all for God. We need to stand firm against the worldviews which exalt the self and desacralizes the Creation, and proclaim that Christ is not *divided*.[7] God is not only above all, but is also *in all* and *through all*.[8] This is preaching a Kingdom of God *at hand*.[9] Making sure you attend church on Sunday morning is not. This is also preaching the *whole* gospel. Preaching individual salvation alone is not preaching the whole gospel. In fact, in the New Testament the gospel is always referred to as the gospel of Kingdom, and Christ himself always refers to it as such.[10] Our collective conscience should reflect the mind and heart of Christ. When Paul teaches about the temple of the Holy Spirit he uses the plural word for *you*. We are not merely individual temples of the Holy Spirit but we are together *one* temple of the Spirit of God. This gives us big challenges in a culture rife with the propagation and advertising of individualism which tells us that we in fact *don't* need each other, *don't* need a community of faith to find truth, and *don't* need any theological traditions to find truth because we can find it within ourselves. Kenneth A. Myers explains that perhaps this is the reason why we have some 20,000 denominations and sects "because of the fact that we have been instilled with this idea that each individual has the capacity to know truth apart from any tradition, apart from

---

[7] 1 Corinthians 10:13
[8] Ephesians 4:6
[9] Matthew 6:33
[10] The one exception is Ephesians 1:13

history, apart from what God has done in the church or in nature."[11] Yet Christ works his power the most manifestly through community and the togetherness of his body. This is why it is so essential for us to understand how "the hand" cannot say to "the foot" that I don't need you, or vice versa.[12] If we continue to focus and centralize our lives inwardly on ourselves we will continue to look more and more like chickens running around with their heads cut off:

> Our kitchens and other eating places more and more resemble filling stations, as our homes more and more resemble motels. Life is not very interesting, we seem to have decided: let its satisfactions be minimal, perfunctory and fast. We hurry through our meals to go to work and hurry through our work in order to recreate ourselves in the evenings and on weekends and vacations, and then we hurry with the greatest possible speed and noise and violence through our recreation. For what? To eat the billionth hamburger at some fast food joint, hell-bent on increasing the quality of our life? And all this is carried out in a remarkable obliviousness to the causes and effects, the possibilities and the purposes of the life of the body in this world.[13]

---

[11] Myers, Kenneth A. "More than Meets the Mouth Or, the Meaning of Meals." *Modern Reformation* "A Feast in a Fast-Food World" July/August Vol. 18 No. 4 (2009): 19-24.

[12] 1 Corinthians 12:15

[13] Wendell Barry. Quoted in "More than Meets the Mouth Or, the Meaning of Meals." By Kenneth A. Meyers. *Modern Reformation*. Issue: "A Feast in a Fast-Food World" July/August Vol. 18 No. 4 2009. Pages 19-24.

INDIVIDUALISM AS AN IDOL

America has such an extreme case of the individualism complex that we now have more people living alone than in any other country in the world.[14] Magazines on the store shelves are all pointing at you as an individual and preaching to you that you should be your own, worry about your own affairs, your looks, your own future. Large corporations mass market their products on the platform that it is all about you. As the worship artist Jason Upton sings in one of his songs, "the greatest idol is you and me...we better get on the threshing floor."[15]

To be like Jesus on the other hand requires a different perspective:

> Yet I do not seek my own glory...
> If I glorify myself, my glory is nothing.[16]

The purpose of God in creating us is that we be a team, one, united in the Spirit of God. This purpose reflects the very nature of God himself and is our testimony of the truth of God to the world:

> Listen O Israel, the Lord is our God, the Lord is one.[17]

God said at the beginning, "It is not good for man to be alone." This is a truth which goes much further and deeper than

---

[14] *NationMaster*. Accessed Aug. 2009 <http://www.nationmaster.com/graph/peo_one_per_hou-people-one-person-households>.
[15] Upton, Jason. "Dying Star." *Dying Star*. Kingsway Music, 2003.
[16] John 8:50; 8:54
[17] Deuteronomy 6:4

merely getting married or enjoying good company. It is a crucial need to be united with others that is inherent in our design as human beings.

God is still at work creating "Adam". He is busy forming millions and millions of children in wombs all across the world right now. He is not yet done with his creating. He was, and is, very serious about man not being alone!

Christ said, "Where two or three are gathered in my name, there I am among them."[18] He never gave any precedence for his power being manifested through one person alone. Indeed, who is anybody by themselves? They are no one. At the day of Christ, Christ will say to many who thought that they could do life on their own: "Depart from me I never knew you"—a bold statement which is to imply that you are a nobody, not even known by God. To seek a loveless, selfish life and not the citizenship of the Kingdom of God is to invite hell. C.S Lewis wrote,

> There is no safe investment. To love at all is to be vulnerable. Love anything, and your heart will certainly be wrung and possibly be broken. If you want to make sure of keeping it intact, you must give your heart to no one, not even an animal. Wrap it carefully round with hobbies and little luxuries; avoid all entanglements; lock it up safe in the casket or coffin of your selfishness. But in that casket — safe, dark, motionless, airless — it will change. It will not be broken; it will become unbreakable, impenetrable, irredeemable. The alternative to tragedy, or at least to the risk of tragedy, is damnation. The only place outside Heaven where you can be perfectly safe from

---

[18] Matthew 18:20

all the dangers and perturbations of love is Hell. I believe that the most lawless and inordinate loves are less contrary to God's will than a self-invited and self-protective lovelessness...We shall draw nearer to God, not by trying to avoid the sufferings inherent in all loves, but by accepting them and offering them to Him; throwing away all defensive armour. If our hearts need to be broken, and if He chooses this as a way in which they should break, so be it. What I know about love and believe about love and giving ones heart began in this.[19]

Lest we begin to think as one of Jean-Paul Sartre's characters in his play *No Exit* that "Hell is other people,"[20] we as American Christians must learn to *die to ourselves* if we are to come out of this culture of individualism and into God's countercultural Kingdom of oneness and loving community through Christ—for we were born, bred, and taught to be self-seeking. It is not going to be a pretty transition for it goes to the deepest place in our being even beyond the culture we were raised in. Most other cultures of the world from the beginning up to the present have had a deeply rooted family system whether it was a clan, tribe, dynasty, kin, brotherhood, or the like. These group identities always took preeminence over self-identity and individualism. It shouldn't be surprising then that the Bible, which exhorts us as a "brotherhood" that partakes of one bread and one cup, is better understood in many of these other cultures.[21]

For us in the Western cultures we think in reverse of this. To disband from family, oneness , and unity, and move toward

---

[19] Lewis, C. S. *The Four Loves*. New York, NY: Brace Harcourt, 1960. p.121
[20] Sartre, Jean-Paul. *No Exit and Three Other Plays*. New York, NY: Vintage Books, 1989.
[21] 1 Peter 2:17, 5:9; 1 Corinthians 10:17

independence, self, and singleness is the lifestyle of our day and is continually commended by the majority. Little or nothing fruitful gets done in this way however. We need accountability. When one of the brotherhood is lifted up by the grace of God to prophetically speak out to certain circumstances in the church like Calvin, Wesley, Fox, or Luther for example, the last thing we need to do as a brotherhood is make them the head of the Church because, as Paul said in Acts, "neither he who plants nor he who waters is anything, but only God gives the growth…He who plants and he who waters are one…"[22] That is a statement which strips the worth of a person's individual achievements, works, and indeed his individuality all together and places it all on God. In other words, they are nothing apart from God who gives the growth. It is not for us to divide ourselves unto who we think has the best interpretations or studies of certain doctrines. What we should do rather is work together as a team where Christ is present! The immeasurable importance of this is revealed in Jesus' own words: "Where two or three are gathered in my name, there I am among them."[23] This truth reflects God's original plan of creating people in such a way that they must rely on, depend on, and need one another rather than the reverse of that. So it is that it is not good for man to be by himself.

We American Christians have a lot of repenting to do. The implications of this Gnostic spirit on us are huge since we are from one of the most broken cultures on the planet with the highest divorce rate in the world,[24] the highest rate of individuals living alone, where more than half of the population of children

---

[22] 1 Corinthians 3:7-8
[23] Matthew 18:20
[24] *NationMaster*. Accessed Aug. 2009
<http://www.nationmaster.com/graph/peo_div_rat-people-divorce-rate>.

come from broken families, and where corporate marketing both feeds and prospers off the idolatry of self. The gospel of the Kingdom has an awesome opportunity to do some major work in such a nation by bringing lost and broken nobodies into a real identity and oneness with God and His family, where they can actually be somebody, rather than being, vainly, the figments of their own imaginations and possessions.

"...you must no longer walk as the Gentiles do, in the futility of their minds!" Ephesians 4:1

Culture of Unspirituality

Now we have received not the spirit of the world, but the Spirit who is from God, that we might understand the things freely given us by God. And we impart this in words not taught by human wisdom but taught by the Spirit, interpreting spiritual truths to those who are spiritual. The natural person does not accept the things of the Spirit of God, for they are folly to him, and he is not able to understand them because they are spiritually discerned. The spiritual person judges all things, but is himself to be judged by no one.
1 Corinthians 2:12-15

An unspiritual culture or society breeds an unspiritual people. This means that as American Christians (with exception to Native Americans) we are born and bred in an unspiritual culture when we come to Christ whereas peoples of many other nations can be of a deeply rooted spiritual culture and thus have a different kind of paradigm to deal with. They may have to fight to come off of polytheism, animism, or witchcraft. Westerners typically have to fight to come off of a bondage to selfish individualism, and an unbelief in the spiritual dimension. People in Islamic countries typically have a deep spiritual foundation of works in place when they come to Christ. There are completely different paradigms that people will struggle to become free of depending on where you come from or what kind of culture you are born in.

The most prevalent attitude in America is likely one of disbelief and criticism of the spiritual altogether. Sue Carran writes,

Americans are not given to understanding spiritual realities, either of the kingdom of God or the kingdom of Satan. Our culture has embraced science and the intellect, through which we interpret all "reality". Yet, the denial of the spiritual realm has created a terrible void in the lives of millions of people because we are created as spiritual beings.[1]

The American's initial attitude to the Spirit of God in our lives will likely be one of "you are out of your minds" whereas a Hindu's initial attitude will likely be "thank you for telling me about another god!" The point that is usually perceived of as folly to the world is the fact that *we have received the Spirit who is from God.* It is a struggle for many in American Christianity to accept this fully. This is a marked reason why so many American Christians lack a life of prayer. Curran notes that in comparison to the rest of the Christian world, American "churches are not overwhelming characterized by a deep dedication to a *committed lifestyle of prayer.* Too many Christians (and even pastors) in our American churches consider prayer an 'option' for seeking supernatural intervention only when our own resourceful initiatives don't seem to be working."[2]

First Corinthians 2:12-15 speaks of the reality of the Spirit in us and how it is to permeate our understanding, our wisdom, our interpretations, our discernment, and our judgment. Sometimes an intelligent mind will divvy up a way to escape and circumvent the reality of this by supposing that the writer was speaking of himself and the specific call and unction given to him to write these Scriptures for us. In effect, the Spirit only speaks to us through Paul. The problem with this is that this is clearly not the

---

[1] Sue Carran, *Prayer in Another Dimension*, (Xulon Press). 2006. p.55
[2] Ibid. p.54

intention of God in giving us his Spirit. Paul as well as the other writers of the New Testament were not called to be mediators like Moses.

God in fact has promised to pour out his Spirit upon all flesh: the old, the young, the sons, the daughters, even the least of society.[3] This very promise poses a problem for the one who would like to have everything under his control. God has chosen in these last days to work directly through each of us by calling each of us to be royal priests under the one high priest, Christ Jesus. Too often however, this is not the case in our churches. The one who is to oversee, feed, and set an example for believers often becomes an exalted priest through whom we all must go through to find God. This is very typical in churches where the role of the Spirit is marginalized or completely compromised. This problem of the exalted priest syndrome was pervasive in the Catholic Church throughout its history. Lust for power and control is a man's greatest temptation. Yet, in spite efforts to counter this through the Reformation, the same problem still exists with Protestantism today. Countless believers won't read the Bible for themselves, or pray and commune with God for themselves—they expect everything to be done for them.

What, then, is the goal of the Christian community? Is it to seek growth? Is it to form grandiose and ambitious plans? Is it to design the perfect model? Is it to live for the community around us? It is neither of these. It is to be spiritual. Jesus says we *must* be spiritually born again if we will enter the Kingdom of God.[4] He calls us to make one thing the primary focus of our seeking hearts. It is not church growth nor great plans or strategies, nor

---

[3] Joel 2:28-29
[4] John 3:3

producing the finest models for fellowship. It is to seek the kingdom of God and his righteousness. Further exposition on what this means leads us ultimately to the Spirit of God. For this kingdom does not consist in talk, food, or drink, but in power, righteousness, joy, and peace *in the Holy Spirit.*

Seeking the Holy Spirit is a duty of every Christian's life. It will lead us into the fruits of the Spirit, and the manifestations of his power. It will not lead us into indecency and chaos, for self-control, order, and peace are his abiding fruits. If someone is compelled to show up to a church service naked, I would hardly consider this a leading of the Holy Spirit. Jesus and his disciples saw this kind of behavior once in a demon-possessed man. If someone ties themselves up as a prophetic act to show what will happen to someone if they depart to a dangerous place, I might consider that the leading of the Holy Spirit. Paul encountered this once.[5] Above all things, the Holy Spirit leads his people to submit to one another, to serve one another, and honor one another.[6] He does not lead us to oppress one another, or control one another, or to argue with one another.[7] Opposition may be a leading of the Spirit, so long as it is done in accordance with the scriptures: with two or three witnesses.[8] Everything is to be done decently and in order.[9]

Consider the emphatic exhortations of the New Testament writers of the life in the Spirit. We are to walk by the Spirit,[10]

---

[5] Acts 21:11
[6] Ephesians 5:21, 1 Peter 4:10, Romans 12:10
[7] 3 John 1:10, 1 Peter 5:3, 1 Timothy 6:4, Titus 3:9
[8] 1 Timothy 5:19
[9] 1 Corinthians 14:40
[10] Galatians 5:16

pray with the Spirit,[11] speak by the Spirit,[12] preach by the Spirit,[13] prophesy by the Spirit,[14] live by the Spirit,[15] partake of the one Spirit,[16] be unified by the Spirit,[17] be reconciled to God by the Spirit,[18] be empowered by the Spirit,[19] be filled with the Spirit,[20] and to serve God by the Spirit.[21] Again, the goal of a Christian community is to seek the Kingdom of God, and the kingdom of God consists of joy, peace, righteousness in the Holy Spirit.[22] If we will ever see revival, we must get our heads out of the anti-spiritual sand of our culture and into the realm of the heavenly Kingdom.

---

[11] Ephesians 6:18, Jude 1:20

[12] 1 Corinthians 12:3,8

[13] 1 Peter 1:12

[14] 1 Samuel 10:6, Joel 2:28, Acts 2:17, 1 Corinthians 14:1

[15] Romans 8:13, Galatians 5:25

[16] 1 Corinthians 12:13

[17] Ephesians 4:3

[18] Ephesians 2:18

[19] 1 Corinthians 12:11

[20] Acts 13:52, Ephesians 5:18

[21] Romans 7:6

[22] Romans 14:17

Culture of
Environmentalism

"...let no one boast in men. For all things are yours, whether Paul or Apollos or Cephas or the world or life or death or the present or the future—all are yours, and you are Christ's, and Christ is God's."
1 Corinthians 3:21-23

The emerging movement of environmentalism has been, more or less, a response to the American pursuit of happiness backfiring on us. It seems that a key point in modern environmentalism is the philosophical postulate of "nonanthropocentrism" which is to say that humanity is not centric to, or any different from, all of the rest of creation. So much for significance. Some mainstream thinking of the day has put emphasis on an "ecocentric" worldview.[1] The hope is to achieve sustainability because nowadays the pursuit of happiness is changing from "consume as much as you can" to "save as much as you can". Yesterday's ignorant hopes in resources have turned into today's panic for lack of resources.

It is interesting to examine how radical these issues in urban environmentalism are, because urban metropolises, megalopolises, and urban sprawl are exploitative by nature. This could perhaps be looked at as a "phenomenon" because no one seems to be in

---

[1] For explanation of Ecocentrism see http://en.wikipedia.org/wiki/Ecocentrism

control of it (even though there is certainly no shortage of complaint to the government to do something about it). It is more a product of the values upon which America is built and which other countries have been following close behind in. They are such values as individual freedom and capitalism. Freedom to consume, freedom to exploit.

Man is like a virus, as it was so eloquently put in the first Matrix movie. They consume and exploit, and then find another place when other areas are exhausted. The building of our urban cities has all been for the singular cause of some kind of "happiness". But that "happiness" turned out to equal "consumption of anything and everything". Of course, we have a problem now because our pursuit has hit a dead end of depleted resources and a whole lot of waste and garbage—something many other societies of the world didn't have time to prepare for and are now suffering from[2]. Now, people are scrambling to back track and find another path. But because it is a product of American values, it would be necessary to deconstruct all the way back to the level of "Life, Liberty, and pursuit of happiness" and then begin a reconstruction of some sort. And how likely is that?

That is why I say to you, don't worry about living - wondering what you are going to eat or drink, or what you are going to wear. Surely life is more important than food, and the body more important than the clothes you wear. Look at the birds in the sky. They never sow nor reap nor store away in barns, and yet your Heavenly Father feeds them. **Aren't you much more valuable to him than they are?** *Can any of you, however much he worries, make himself an inch taller?*

---

[2] For example, Zabaleen, Cairo. <http://en.wikipedia.org/wiki/Zabbaleen>

And why do you worry about clothes? Consider how the wild flowers grow. They neither work nor weave, but I tell you that even Solomon in all his glory was never arrayed like one of these! Now if God so clothes the flowers of the field, which are alive today and burnt in the stove tomorrow, is he not much more likely to clothe you, you 'little-faiths'?

So don't worry and don't keep saying, 'What shall we eat, what shall we drink or what shall we wear?! That is what pagans are always looking for; your Heavenly Father knows that you need them all. Set your heart on the kingdom and his goodness, and all these things will come to you as a matter of course.

Jesus (Matthew 6:25-33 Phillips)

As a child of the Creator and Sustainer of all life, we have a responsibility for creation. It is here to teach us and lead us to the One who made it. Even the scriptures themselves were written for our sake.[3] When Christ came in the flesh, he taught and spoke to us using creation for symbols and allegories. We learn about providence through the flowers and the birds.[4] We learn about his kingly strength and boldness through the lion.[5] We learn about humility and obedience through the sheep.[6] We learn about prideful individualism and disobedience through the goat.[7] We learn about judgment through the wheat and the weeds.[8] We learn about false teachers and prophets through the wolf.[9] We

---

[3] John 12:30; 1 Corinthians 9:9-10; Romans 4:23
[4] Matthew 6:25-33
[5] Hosea 5:14; Revelation 5:5; Proverbs 28:1
[6] John 10:3-4
[7] Matthew 25:33
[8] Matthew 13:30
[9] Matthew 7:15; Acts 20:29

learn about the words we speak and the deeds of the Holy Spirit through fruit.[10] We understand the redemption and forgiveness of sins through water.[11] The whole of creation speaks praise to the Lord—the sun, the moon, the stars, the creatures of the ocean, the fire, the hail, the snow, the rain, the mountains, the trees, the wild animals, and the livestock.[12] We learn that we are to lead creation in that praise, being the only creation made in the very image of God.[13]

The Bible states that the meek will inherit the earth,[14] and it should be noted that it is not the other way around. There is an order in which everything is set, so that we may gain knowledge of the truth by the things that are made.[15]

---

[10] Matthew 7:18, 12:33; Galatians 5:22
[11] Matthew 3:11
[12] Psalm 148
[13] Genesis 1:26
[14] Matthew 5:5
[15] Romans 1:20

We call upon the mountains
The Cascades and the Olympics
The high green valleys
And meadows filled with wild flowers
The snow that never melt
The summits of intense silence
And we ask that they teach us, and show us the Way

We call upon the forests
The great trees reaching strongly to the sky
With earth in their roots
And the heavens in their branches
The fir and the pine and the cedar
And we ask them to teach us, and show us the Way.
- Chinook Indian Invocation

"I am the Way, the Truth, and the Life."
- Jesus

Lovers of Money

"Too many of us look upon Americans as dollar chasers. This is a cruel libel, even if it is reiterated thoughtlessly by the Americans themselves."
Albert Einstein

No servant can serve two masters, for either he will hate the one and love the other, or he will be devoted to the one and despise the other. You cannot serve God and money. Luke 14:13

There's no question about how much we love money. Americans *love* money. So much so that *time* itself has become equated with money, and as a result our entire lives as Americans have become structured around this principle. Community, also, is being redefined in terms of the shopping mall.[1] As money rises and falls, inflates and deflates, so goes the American mood. Americans will even go so far as to spend money they don't have. As of 2009, Americans have spent themselves into 2.5 trillion dollars of debt—and it continues to grow.[2] Says CNN, "The American consumer has become deeply addicted to spending."[3]

---

[1] Lynn A. Staeheli; Don Mitchell. "USA's destiny? Regulating space and creating community in American Shopping Malls." *Urban Studies* 1360-063X, Volume 43, Issue 5, 2006, pp. 977 – 992
[2] United States Federal Reserve. *Consumer Credit*. Aug. 2009. Accessed 16 Aug. 2009 <http://www.federalreserve.gov/releases/g19/hist/cc_hist_sa.html>.
[3] Lahart, Justin. "Spending our way to disaster." 3 Oct. 2003. CNNMoney.com. Accessed 16 Aug. 2009 <http://money.cnn.com/2003/10/02/markets/consumerbubble/>.

Since the early days of America's history people have ever been in a rush for the "gold". Where there is money to be had, the people go mad. One of the last big "gold" rushes in America was the internet "dot.com rush"[4] in which every entrepreneur (and their mothers) was rushing to cash in on the explosion of the domain market and website businesses. You can observe other gold rushes happening now as social websites like Myspace.com and Facebook.com become the most visited and used websites on the planet. Everyone is trying to cash in on the new market with gadgets, bells and whistles, and everything in between. High internet website traffic is the "black gold" of today and if you can tap into that you can get yourself some great advertising potential which translates into cash in your pocket.

Jesus said that no one can serve two masters. You will either hate God and love money (or something else), or you will be devoted to God and despise money. The scripture then goes on to say that the hypocrite Pharisees, who were lovers of money, ridiculed Jesus.[5] From this standpoint alone, we can see why bringing the Way of Jesus into the American way of life is often taken as a ridiculous idea. Just talk a little bit about money, faith, and the lordship of Christ in almost any group of self-reliant American Christians and you will undoubtedly be met with frowning faces and disapproval. While many go to and fro seeking after fame and cash, those who choose to cast off the bondage of pursuing wealth and despise it are often ridiculed by the rest. There is perhaps no point of Christian doctrine or belief

---

[4] Anderson, Kevin. "Dot.com gold rush ends." *BBC News: Business* 30 May 2000: 1 BBC Newsonline. Accessed 6 Aug. 2009 <http://news.bbc.co.uk/2/hi/business/766098.stm>.
[5] Luke 16:13-15

as contradictory to the American way of life as this. You're told that you're foolish if you don't spend your life to get a good enough job to live the American "dream" of materialistic lust. You're told, "If you don't get an education you'll be poor, and you certainly don't want to be poor!" Even well meaning Christians can miss the point with the thought that unless you have "nice" things, God has not really provided for your "needs".

It is true that God wants to bless us and pour out his abundant goodness upon us. He provides for our food and clothing and shelter. He is gracious with these things even. At times, there is wine and tasty bread to be had from his hand. The problem is not whether one has money and nice things or not. The problem is our slavery to them. We are enslaved to all the good things, and Christ came to set us free.

We American Christians will make all kinds of excuses to try to justify what is really our enslavement. True, God is not calling us to be ascetics or like John the Baptist, and true, God delights to provide everything we need and sometimes even more. But to take that truth and use it as an excuse for your love of money and things is no better than defending your bondage to them.

Christ encountered the rich young ruler and told him to sell everything he had and then follow him.[6] The point here was not that this rich man was sinning by having riches and prestige, but rather that his heart needed to be loosed from them. That is why Christ told him to go sell it all. It literally takes just that kind of sacrifice to be free from things that will hold us in bondage. If we are not free from them, we cannot follow Christ, and if we cannot follow Christ, we are none of his disciples. It was the same kind of request that God gave to Abraham when he told him to

---

[6] Mark 10:17-23

go up on a hill and sacrifice Isaac. There had to be a real willingness that manifests itself before there is real freedom. Faith without works is dead. In these situations the Holy Spirit is seen to work powerfully.[7]

Despite the New Testament teaching of generous giving, Christians are not quick to let go of their money—perhaps because of a widespread lack of generosity or distrust for organized religious institutions. According to the Barna Group, among all born-again adults only 9% offered any more than a tenth of their income. Interestingly, Christians still give more than anyone else.[8]

Motivations for work, school, business, politics, innovation, creativity, etc. which stem from a root of love for money will produce all kinds of evil,[9] and will only be to your shame. For those seeking the Kingdom of God, and not money, the pursuit of education, work, business, politics, innovation, creativity, etc. stems from a love of God, and will produce good and abiding fruit to the glory of God and your joy. After his bold declarations to the lovers of money, Jesus makes an even more bold declaration saying, "For what is exalted among men is an abomination in the sight of God."[10] With a declaration like that, you can get a pretty clear idea of how far and wide the gap is between the exalted, money-centered American way of life and serving God, and how great a folly it is to try to serve both—something many Christians try to do.

---

[7] Acts 4:32-37

[8] "New Study Shows Trends in Tithing and Donating." Barna Group. 14 Apr. 2008. 14 Aug. 2009 <http://www.barna.org/barna-update/article/18-congregations/41-new-study-shows-trends-in-tithing-and-donating>.

[9] 1 Timothy 6:10

[10] Luke 14:15

Christianity and Consumerism

The rise of consumerism since World War II has had a pervasive and profound impact on the Christian faith of the West that is changing some of the most fundamental and foundational values of the Christian Church. The typical church agenda for helping the needy and oppressed, seeking unity in diversity, and finding spiritual identity has been replaced by agendas for defending the middle class and wealthy, growth through target marketing, and buying into consumer identities. What is in effect happening is a paradoxical battle between charitable mentality and indulgent mindlessness.

A NEW ECONOMY OF SALVATION

To illustrate the acuteness of the change taking place, Martin E. Marty, a writer for the Christian Century Magazine, argues that the ancient phrase and idea of an "economy of salvation" which referred to divine stewardship has been supplanted by a different meaning—one of many choices or marketing for something "cheap". Two particular strategies of church growth are compared to show the contrasting ideas:

> The first offers an economy of salvation on the cheap...let people know that 'all are welcome'; 'come as you are' implies

that there will never be demands...Yes, there are some prices: church members have to give generously. But in this economy God promises commensurate rewards...The second offers an economy of salvation that is expensive. There is more biblical warrant if less marketing finesse in this approach. Dietrich Bonhoeffer called it The Cost of Discipleship, picking up on Jesus' stories that command, for the sake of the kingdom, that we sell all that we have and give to the poor.[1]

In an editorial from the Irish Independent, the battle is seen as one religion clashing with a new pseudo-religion of consumerism:

> You become a consumerist when you start to believe 'I buy, therefore I am', and to think, 'I am what I buy'. Everyone needs something on which to hang their identity, from which to derive a sense of meaning and purpose. That sense used to come from belonging to a particular religion, or a tribe, or a nation, or a clan or some combination of all these things. But modern individualism encourages us to construct our identity, our sense of meaning, for ourselves, and that's where consumerism comes in. It encourages us to construct an image for ourselves from the things we buy, an image we can then present to the world for its judgment...The true consumerist, the true victim of affluenza, always views themselves through the eyes of others. The advertisers are their priests, telling them how to live their lives and construct their sense of self. Advertisements are their catechism and their fellow consumerists are their fellows believers. It is they [who] will judge them and place them among the consumerist saints, or

---

[1] Marty, Martin E., "Bagged for Jesus", Christian Century 10/16/2007, Vol. 124 Issue 21, p71

sinners according to how successfully they have built their image.[2]

Descartes concept of 'I think, therefore I exist' is now giving way to the new postmodern-consumer-way of thinking, 'I buy, therefore I exist'. Forget about the hailed 'purpose driven life', we have the more imminent problem of the 'purchase driven life' to deal with.

Following the World War II era, large suburban communities began to sprout overnight along with the entrance of mega-malls and shopping centers. While this was going on, two significant things have occurred. Firstly, the value of the traditional identity in family was engulfed and wiped out by the value of a new consumer individual identity. As an individual consumer, you are free to define yourself and write your own life story. In a study on consumption and identity Peter Jackson notes, "identity is a reflexive project...sustained through narratives of the self...Consumption can play a vital role in the articulation of such narratives."[3] The interesting thing to note here is that this self-directed and self-made narrative in the new consumer society is dependent on the amount of money you have. Secondly, there was a great migration of middle and wealthy class people to the suburbs. The shopping center suburbs have provided a utopic hope for anyone—so long as you have the money—to realize the American Dream of individualism. What makes this significant is that these middle class and wealthy families that once filled the cities were predominately white. When many African Americans

---

[2] "Affluenza is new religion and its creed is spend, spend, spend" Sept. 2006: Irish Independent http://www.independent.ie/opinion/editorial/affluenza-is-new-religion-and-its-creed-is-spend-spend-spend-77455.html
[3] Jackson, Peter, "Consumption and Identity", European Planning Studies, 7:1, 1999. p.29

moved out of the south into the major cities, the middle class moved out of the cities to the suburbs. In fact, suburbia was designed to favor the white middle-class men, as the mortgages, credit, and tax benefits were catered to them.[4] The poorer, who could not afford to live in the suburbs, had to find their places within the city where it was cheaper. In A Consumer Republic, Lizabeth Cohen writes, "Race was intrinsic to the process of postwar suburbanization, as the steady influx of African Americans to northern and western cities during the war, and the Second Great Migration out of the South that followed it, helped motivate urban whites to leave."[5]

Since this shift took root after World War II, the Christian Church has found itself facing one of the biggest disharmonies in its history. Looking further into the specific studies done on the subject, we find that not only has this consumerism and individualism affected the Christian church, but has in fact left it ethnically fragmented and divided. Paul Metzger argues in his provocative book *Consuming Christianity* that a major factor of consumerism's effects within the Christian community has to do with race and class divisions: "the approach taken by the Religious Right, the Moral Majority, the Christian Coalition, and the like over the last few decades...exemplifies an adherence to political and social policies that give the appearance of being fixated on conservative, middle class American social values."[6] He goes on to say that "many evangelical leaders give the appearance of going to battle to maintain...a certain standard of living and

---

[4] Cohen, Lizabeth. *A Consumer's Republic: The Politics of Mass Consumption in Postwar America* (New York, Vintage Books, 2003), p.200

[5] Ibid. p.212

[6] Metzger, Paul Louis. *Consuming Jesus* (Grand Rapids, MI, William B. Eerdmans Publishing Company, 2007), p.33

way of life—even a Kinkadian-like utopian vision of upward mobility and homogeneity."[7] Through pragmatism as well as political reductionism, many evangelical leaders have given up trying to bring unity and diversity to their churches and communities and have instead settled for what seems to work best and brings in the most people. No longer is the lobbying or defense equally for all—including those who are poor, orphaned, widowed, oppressed, downtrodden, homeless., etc, but increasingly exclusive to those who are prosperous and well-off in the suburbs.[8]

CHURCH GROWTH

Looking back on the new meaning that "economy of salvation" has taken on in the 20th century, the question of church growth comes to mind. What are the implications of the 'new economy of salvation' on church growth? In reference to the American economy, Lizabeth Cohen quotes Jack Isidor Straus, the board chairman of Macy's in 1963, as proclaiming, "Our economy keeps growing because our ability to consume is endless."[9] The more consumerism there is the more apparent growth. As waves of people began buying meaning and identity for themselves as individuals, the temptation to get in on the market was too much for churches to resist. As a result, target marketing and reductionism has become part and parcel to church growth, and the path of least resistance has become 'the

---

[7] Ibid. p.33
[8] Ibid. p.25, 28
[9] Lizabeth Cohen, *A Consumer's Republic*, p.261

way, the truth, and the life' while little consideration is given to those outside the target groups.

Marketing is not the same as publicizing. In the book *Marketing for Congregations* it states that "Marketing is not selling, advertising, or promotion…Marketing is the analysis, planning, implementation, and control of carefully formulated programs to bring about voluntary 'exchanges' with specifically targeted groups for the purpose of achieving the organization's missional objectives."[10] But is this core of the Christian conviction and the mission of the Church? Philip Kenneson and James Street remind us that the core of our conviction and mission is self-denial and sacrifice because salvation and the Holy Spirit are God's *gifts* to us:

> The concept of gift is critically central to the logic of Christian convictions. But when we view the entire world through the marketing lens, the notion of gift disappears. Should Christians be so willing to give up on the notion of "gift," replacing it instead with the concept of self-interested exchange? We believe that replacing the concept of gift with that of exchange corrupts our relationship with God and our relationships with other people.[11]

We come to God with absolutely nothing to bring in exchange for his presence in our lives. If our relationship with God is not based on self-interested exchange but is his *free gift*, then clearly our relationships with others and with the Church should not be either.

---

[10] Norman Shawchuck, Philip Kotler, Bruce Wrenn, and Gustave Rath, *Marketing for Congregations: Choosing to Serve People More Effectively* (Nashville: Abingdon Press, 1992), p. 43.

[11] Philip D. Kenneson, James L. Street, *Selling Out the Church: The Dangers of Church Marketing* (Eugene, Or: Cascade Books, 1997), *p. 49.*

In his book The McDonaldization of the Church, John Drane juxtaposes the well-known thesis of "the McDonaldization of Society"[12] to the modern Christian evangelical Church and seeks to show us that this social and structural change in society is also happening in the Christian community. The concept of "the McDonaldization of Society" was coined by sociologist George Ritzer in 1993 and referred to "the process by which the principles of the fast-food restaurants are coming to dominate more and more sectors of American society as well as of the rest of the world."[13] Ritzer explained that these principles can be traced back to Henry Ford's methods of the assembly line and mass production where complicated tasks were broken down into many smaller and simpler ones. Efficiency was the key to success. These methods were later adopted by Ray Kroc, the founder of McDonald's to break down hamburger cooking into a precise and efficient process.

The effect of "McDonaldization" can be seen everywhere. Sociologist Michael Farrall from St. Edwards University responding to Ritzer's work writes, "this process, occurring throughout society, is transforming our lives. Shopping malls are controlled environments of approved design, logo, colors, and opening and closing hours. Travel agencies transport middle-class Americans to ten European capitals in fourteen days, each visitor experiencing exactly the same hotels, restaurants, and other predictable settings. No one need fear meeting a "real" native. USA Today produces the same bland, instant news - in short,

---

[12] Ritzer, George, *The McDonaldization of Society*, (Pine Forge Press, 1993).
[13] Ibid. p.1

unanalytic pieces that can be read between gulps of the McShake or the McBurger."[14]

Four points are made by Ritzer as to the effects of McDonaldization in society: efficiency, calculability, predictability, and control. According to Drane it is the dimension of predictability that has transformed the Church the most:

> "of the four major traits of McDonaldization identified by Ritzer, this is the one which is most easily identified in the Church. Ritzer defines it in the following terms:
> In a rational society people prefer to know what to expect in all settings and at all times. They neither want nor expect surprises... In order to ensure predictability over time and place, a rational society emphasizes such things as discipline, order, systematization, formalization, routine, consistency, and methodical operation... It is these familiar and comfortable rituals that make fast-food restaurants attractive to legions of people."[15]

One of the main dysfunctions of the McDonaldized, predictable church is the increasing importance of quantity over quality. When quantity becomes the rule of thumb by which the success of a church is measured it can very easily become the agenda leaving little room for quality. In effect, members become mass produced through means of prepackaged and highly pragmatic methods that are targeted towards the demographic that will bring the most numbers. Ritzer argues that the

---

[14] Farrall, Michael. "The McDonaldization of Society." <http://myweb.stedwards.edu/mikef/mcdonize.htm>. Accessed 27 May 2008.
[15] Drane, John, *The McDonaldization of the Church: Consumer Culture and the Church's Future* (Smyth & Helwy's Publishing Inc., 2001), p.48

"rationality" of these processes are ultimately irrational. He writes, "Most specifically, irrationality means that rational systems are unreasonable systems. By that I mean that they deny the basic humanity, the human reason, of the people who work within or are served by them."[16] Such methodical processes for producing high growth not only yield products of cheap quality, but undermine basic humanity and human reason. The difference can be as wide as a handmade product versus a mass-produced one. As Drane states, "There is a widespread tendency today to equate quality with quantity in many different areas of life....Christians are not immune from this obsession with numbers and quantity."[17] As the core values of the Church begin to revolve more around quantity, many Christians are beginning to question the leadership and cast doubt on their abilities and motives. Many Christians have also left the Church in untold numbers due to these problems.[18] But if church agendas and success are become quantity centered, other values begin to emerge. "The issue of power and control is at the heart of all the other factors that are at work in a McDonaldized style of being...Numbers become all-important to church leaders, especially in the American context where churches are self-consciously competing with one another for market share, because they endow clergy with status both in the local situation and also in the wider denominational contexts."[19] Drawing a connection between motives in numbers and the dawning of consumer individual identity, we find a strong sense that church

---

[16] Ritzer, George, *The McDonaldization of Society,* p.154

[17] Drane, John. *The McDonaldization of the Church*, p.44

[18] Jamieson, Alan. A *Churchless Faith: Faith Journeys Beyond the Churches* (Pilgrim Press, 2002).

[19] Drane, John, The *McDonaldization of the Church,* p.54

leaders are seeking their own consumer identities incited by new ideals of church leadership. There is in addition to consumerism among the lay people of society a consumerism within the realm of leadership. Religious and academic status are ascribed to the number of books you write and sell, the number of sermons you preach, the number of lay people in your pew, and even how many possessions you own. However, as the "out-of-church" Christian movement suggests, this is not working very well. In the short-run the marketing seems to work, but as Alan Jamieson points out, most "out-of-church Christians" have left a church they've been a member of for over 15 years.[20] In the long-run, the effort to process prepackaged models and mass-marketing schemes to gain numbers is having adverse effects.

The concept of target-marketing in church practice is discussed at length by Metzger. Reaching out to the community for the sake of the gospel requires an attitude of inclusion or what is sometimes referred to as "contextualization". He argues however, that contextualization and demographic targeting are not the same. To embark on a path towards a specific demographic is to "militate against whole-person and whole-community analysis...". Metzger goes on to say, "I would hate to be the person attending a purpose-driven church who comes to the realization that he is not the kind of person that the church is targeting. The fact that my likings are different might very well mean that the church might not really like me."[21] This very issue brings us full circle to the problem of consumer market segmentation and the class and race divisions it has unknowingly promoted.

---

[20] Jamieson, Alan, *A Churchless Faith*.
[21] Metzger, Paul Louis, *Consuming Jesus*, p.53

THE SUBURBAN CHURCH

The suburban church especially has found success—as far as numbers go—through McDonaldization where individualism and consumerism reign. Going back to Metzger's study, our attention is turned to John Perkins, an African American evangelical Christian leader speaking for the inner city working class minorities who asserts that many churches "have substituted a gospel of church growth for a gospel of reconciliation...so the most segregated racist institution in America, the evangelical church, racks up the numbers...oblivious to the fact [of] the dismemberment of the body of Christ..."[22] It appears the movement has been more toward isolation than toward inclusion. In a recent study it was found that in the last couple of decades American's have found themselves with fewer real friends or confidants outside the family.[23] "The study paints a picture of Americans' social contacts as a "densely connected, close, homogeneous set of ties slowly closing in on itself, becoming smaller, more tightly interconnected, more focused on the very strong bonds of the nuclear family. That means fewer contacts created through clubs, neighbors and organizations outside the home".[24] The same study also revealed social network stratification according to race and class. Through the paths of least resistance, churches have isolated and stratified themselves much in the same way where fewer and fewer contacts are made outside the church as well as between races and classes.

---

[22] Ibid. p.9
[23] Hicks, Sally, "Americans Have Fewer Friends Outside the Family, Duke Study Shows", June 2006.
http://www.dukenews.duke.edu/2006/06/socialisolation.html
[24] Ibid.

For decades the Christian Church has been deeply affected by the trends and movements of consumerism and its insatiable desires for more. What this means for the Church's future is uncertain but perhaps closely related to the future of the consumer society at large to which it seems to be vehemently attached. The patterns of consumer society have lured the best of churches as the polarization of the suburbs and cities widen, and the means of growth McDonaldize.

The epidemic is global. When traditional and religious values come into contact with consumerism and capitalism, the offspring becomes a diffused mix of each with capitalism being the dominate value. The scene in China is a good foreign representation of the patterns found here in America. Bin Zhao writes,

In today's China, pragmatism has triumphed over other ideologies; the quintessence of this stance is captured in Deng Xiaoping's "cat theory"—"it does not matter whether the cat is white or black, as long as it catches the mice, it is a good cat." For most people, it no longer matters whether the cat is "socialism with Chinese characteristics" or "capitalism with Confucian colours." As long as it works for China's development, it is regarded as a "good-ism".[25]

If the Confucian community intermingled with capitalism and begat "capitalism with Confusion colors" as Zhao states, then what can be said for the Christian Church intermingling with it? In a general point of view from the issues discussed it very much appears like capitalism with Christian colors.

---

[25] Bin Zhao, "Consumerism, Confucianism, Communism: Making Sense of China Today", New Left Review, Vol. A, March 1997.

Land and Possessions

The earth is the Lord's, and everything in it, the world, and all who live in it. Psalm 24:1

When the churches of the earlier days were formed it was no big deal to buy up a plot of land and build a massive edifice on it, for land and resources were generally available in abundance at cheap prices. Due to the phenomenon of urban sprawl and the expansion of metropolitan commuter mega-cities, today's churches face a dilemma with this tradition of buying private property. Property values are expensive and taxes are high. Land is very difficult to obtain except by the middle and upper classes, even on the outskirts of urban centers. It has become a luxury reserved to the wealthy to own a sizable plot of land anymore. Yet the tradition of churches buying and owning property still trudges on and nowadays churches are paying in the millions of dollars to make their dreams of property ownership and personal sanctuary design possible. Rather than reusing old church edifices (which more often than not are in prime locations), we have chosen to go after massive building projects of new church buildings, usually on the outskirts of urban centers where there is still a little bit of land remaining but usually costing no small sum of money. Meanwhile, the countless church buildings already in existence are considered outmoded, irrelevant, and undesirable. Consequently, they are abandoned, torn down, or sold to entrepreneurs who turn them into pubs and theaters.

This leaves us with a pressing question: Is this the kind of stewardship example we want to set for the world? As it is now, a lot of money seems to be wasted. Our stewardship is not good.

More and more of our resources are being spent to suit our "felt needs" and personal interests. A Chinese missionary, after touring churches in the United States, is quoted as saying, "I am amazed at how much the Church in America can accomplish without the Holy Spirit."[1] Indeed when giving in the American Protestant Church alone amounts to around 17 billion dollars annually[2], a lot can be accomplished. But what exactly is being accomplished?

Research done by Generous Giving Inc. revealed that 31 percent of pastors said they'd build up their church buildings in the event of a financial windfall, while 7 percent said they would give more to outreach and missions. On average, 50% of a church's budget goes to salaries while 5% goes to missions or outreach. An average of 22% of a church's budget is spent on building maintenance or expansion. Only 2% of what American Christians give go to overseas ministries. All in all, about 85% of all church spending is directed inwardly.[3]

Buildings are available everywhere for us to use but because the pursuit and aim of our churches has turned into more of a consumerist aim for happiness and pleasure, church leaders are giving in to scratching people's itching ears...and backsides. People want a bigger and better sound system so we give it to them. They want more plushy seats so we give it to them. People want a coffee lounge, so we give it to them. They want a basketball gym, so we give it to them. But is this the Way of Jesus? At the same time, protestant giving is at an all time low

[1] Sue Carran, *Prayer in Another Dimension*, (Xulon Press). 2006. p.54-55
[2] Guthrie, Stan. "Giving: Protestant Giving Rates Decline." *Christianity Today.* Mar. 2001. Accessed 23 Sep. 2009 <http://www.christianitytoday.com/ct/2001/march5/9.21.html>.
[3] *Generous Giving*. Accessed 23 Sep. 2009 <http://www.generousgiving.org/stats>.

percentage-wise and while American Christians are the most generous givers in the nation, we are by no means making sacrifices. The American Church is only giving 2.5% of their income when we hold 80% of the evangelical world's wealth.[4] If this is the case, then we are far from showing ourselves as cheerful givers. Perhaps American Christians aren't as excited about the coziness and comforts of church gyms and lounges as we think.

Meanwhile, God has been always been vigilant about expressing to us his heart for the poor and his will for us to be his hands and feet to them:

Is it not to share your bread with the hungry and bring the homeless poor into your house; when you see the naked, to cover him, and not to hide yourself from your own flesh? Then shall your light break forth like the dawn, and your healing shall spring up speedily; your righteousness shall go before you; the glory of the Lord shall be your rear guard. Then you shall call, and the Lord will answer; you shall cry, and he will say, 'Here I am.' If you take away the yoke from your midst, the pointing of the finger, and speaking wickedness, if you pour yourself out for the hungry and satisfy the desire of the afflicted, then shall your light rise in the darkness and your gloom be as the noonday. And the Lord will guide you continually and satisfy your desire in scorched places and make your bones strong; and you shall be like a watered garden, like a spring of water, whose waters do not fail. Isaiah 58:7-11

And Jesus, looking at him, loved him, and said to him, "You lack one thing: go, sell all that you have and give to the poor, and you will

---

[4] John Ronsvalle and Sylvia Ronsvalle, The State of Church Giving through 2004: Will We Will? 16th ed. (Champaign, Ill.: Empty Tomb, 2006).

have treasure in heaven; and come, follow me." Disheartened by the saying, he went away sorrowful, for he had great possessions. Mark 10:21-22

Jesus most certainly was not an advocate for the accumulation of possessions. If we preach this principle to individuals, are we practicing it as a church also? As leaders serving Jesus, we need to be teaching people to set their minds on things above,[5] and to desiring the heavenly things of God. We need to be teaching them to be a people after God's own heart who desires the welfare of the poor, lame, blind, and destitute. We need to teach them to desire God's kingdom and righteousness.[6] In short, we need to be teaching them to desire the things that *Jesus* desires. The grave warning to us in this regard is the fact that we who become teachers of the gospel will be judged with greater strictness.[7]

---

[5] Colossians 3:2
[6] Matthew 6:33
[7] James 3:1

Christian Pharisees

The scribes and the Pharisees sit on Moses seat, so practice and observe whatever they tell you—but not what they do. For they preach, but do not practice. Matthew 23:2-3

Pharisaism is defined as a hypocritical observance of the letter of religious or moral law without regard for the spirit, which is what the Pharisees of Jesus' day were known for. Jesus taught his disciples to avoid following them, for they were dangerous. He also taught that because they sit on the Word of God, their instruction should be heeded. The Pharisees had such a bad example that Jesus went so far as to teach that they would cross land and sea to make a single proselyte only to make him twice as much a child of hell as themselves.[1] Truly the spirit of Pharisaism still persists today.

The modern Church, regardless of denomination, has its Pharisees. It is not just a problem of a Jewish sect a couple thousand years ago. It is a reality and darkness within the ranks and walls of the Church today. Thus did Jesus preach and teach so fervently about it. We have to notice how Christ responded to these kind of people, so that we do not become like them in our own temptations to sin. One of the greatest cautions he teaches is to not become like them. Too often the spirit of bitterness can take a hold of a believer's life because of some preacher's hypocritical example. It is all too easy to become hypocritical ourselves on account of hypocrites yet Jesus never condemned

---

[1] Matthew 23:15

them nor judged them, as he did not come to judge the world.[2] He warned his followers not to do what they did or follow their example. Instead, he instructed them to take what they had to teach and carry on. Do not follow them. You will find that Jesus never ate or dined with them but instead preferred hanging out with sinners and prostitutes.[3] Just a little leaven of the Pharisees, and the whole loaf would be stained.

"Beware of the leaven of the Pharisees, which is hypocrisy. Nothing is covered up that will not be revealed, or hidden that will not be known. Therefore whatever you have said in the dark shall be heard in the light, and what you have whispered in private rooms shall be proclaimed on the housetops." Jesus, Luke 12:1-3

A major principle of the Christian walk is patient endurance.[4] Hypocrites will come, and there will be plenty of them, but *do not become like them.* Resist the temptations, and be wise as serpents and gentle as doves. If we accuse, condemn, or condescend, we become like them. If we become puffed up, haughty, self-righteous, or put our spirituality on display for man's approval, we become like them. If we show partiality, we become like them. If we boast that we can do ministry better than them, we deceive ourselves and become like them.

Moreover, they sit on the right seat, not the wrong seat. They are not heretics, nor teachers of a false religion. They are preachers of the true Word of God. Therefore, Jesus' warning is

---

[2] John 8:15; 12:47
[3] John 8:3-11; Matthew 21:28-32; Luke 5:29-32
[4] Luke 21:19; Romans 5:7; Hebrews 10:36; Revelation 1:9, 2:2, 3:10

not that the disciples shouldn't listen to them, but that they should not *be like them.*

BE ANGRY, DO NOT SIN

We are exhorted to be angry without sinning. Part of building our character in Christ is learning how to express a righteous anger. Most people have no problem with expressing sinful anger, but a righteous anger is one borne from the Spirit of God within us. Its fruit is the exaltation of the righteousness of God and not our own righteousness, and, in many cases, conviction and repentance on part of the hearers. Jesus' examples of righteous anger were always in response to the hypocrisy of his day.[5] We too can, and should, express a holy anger with hypocritical actions of those who call themselves brothers. Paul, in a dramatic demonstration of what it really means to love your brothers fiercely, confronted Peter *to his face* in front of everybody when Peter slipped into hypocritical behavior:

But when Cephas came to Antioch, I opposed him to his face, because he stood condemned. For before certain men came from James, he was eating with the Gentiles; but when they came he drew back and separated himself, fearing the circumcision party. And the rest of the Jews acted hypocritically along with him, so that even Barnabas was led astray by their hypocrisy. But when I saw that their conduct was not in step with the truth of the gospel, I said to Cephas before them

---

[5] John 2:13-17; Mark 3:1-6

all, "If you, though a Jew, live like a Gentile and not like a Jew, how can you force the Gentiles to live like Jews?" Galatians 2:11-14

Hypocrisy is not to be taken lightly and should not be tolerated in the Church. Within the house of the Lord, it must be confronted and overturned, even as Jesus overturned the tables of robbery and hypocrisy in his Father's temple. It is not an easy task to be in Paul's position before reputable preachers and Christian leaders. To stand for what is right sometimes means to risk your neck. Just ask Jesus. However, we are all sinners, and we all are tempted to hypocrisy. Therefore beware and be quick to repent whenever you catch yourself saying or doing something hypocritical! Do not let the sun go down on your anger. Forgive those who mistreated you or neglected you on account of your racial background, your educational background, your financial background, your family background, or your job background. Forgive so that you will be forgiven your own sins! If you have shown partiality in your church or your ministry and have excluded or repressed people because of their racial background, or their educational background, or their family background, or their financial background, or their job background, you are just like the Pharisees. A hypocrite! You have polluted the table of the Lord with hypocritical offerings, and have neglected justice, mercy, and faithfulness! Repent and heed the words of the Lord as spoken by Malachi:

For the lips of a priest should guard knowledge, and people should seek instruction from his mouth, for he is the messenger of the Lord *of hosts. But you have turned aside from the way. You have caused many to stumble by your instruction. You have corrupted the covenant of Levi, says the* Lord *of hosts, and so I make you despised and abased before all the people, inasmuch as you do not keep my ways but show partiality in your instruction." Malachi 2:7-9*

Peter himself fell victim to this most wretched sin, and stood condemned. Yet he persevered through the accountability of others because the grace of Jesus was more powerful in his life than the sin, and he is remembered as the Apostle Peter, a founder of the Church.

Redefining Missions

America has seen many shifts in the understanding of the concept of Missions. It seems that as the "mission field" changes, so does the meaning of the word itself. And so it should. Missions is contextualizing and going into the world with the news of Jesus Christ. It is always new. It is initiating a battle with darkness. Most of all, it is an act of faith for the glory of God, for anything not done from faith is sin[1], and the very work of God is to be constantly walking by faith.[2]

For our purposes, what we will refer to here as "missions" is what James Hudson Taylor III referred to as "the Word of God spread". The living Word is not merely a sequence of letters and syllables; it is the second person of the triune godhead. It is God-speak. It is Spirit. It is alive and active.[3] Imagine what it would be like if people could not speak words—in a philosophical sense, people would not exist. Essentially, people are 'little words' whereas God is *the* Word[4], and it is in his image that all of us 'little words' were made.[5] This is one reason why it is so important that we take care with the words we speak.[6] Therefore, we are looking at something much larger than just 'missions'. We are looking at the spreading of the Word of God which is Christ. When we reexamine 1 Corinthians 3:10-16, we find that this is

---

[1] Romans 14:23
[2] John 6:29
[3] Hebrews 4:12
[4] John 1:1-14
[5] Hebrews 11:3
[6] Matthew 12:36-37

not merely evangelism, preaching, or delivering scriptures. It is something that is planted and is alive and active.

It is alive and active because a living foundation is laid by those so gifted and called[7]—a foundation of the living word upon which people are built up into a 'temple'.[8] It is the Word of life and thus imparts life to the people.[9] It is what we preach and speak.[10] It is, at essence, Jesus Christ himself.[11] It is not a physical building after the shadow of the Old Testament, but the reality: a building made of people.

This mandate is the blessing of Abraham.[12] The body of Christ is gifted to carry and spread this blessing by planting these foundations in places where they have not been planted. It is a gifting that enables us to reveal the mysteries of God and lay the foundations of the spiritual buildings of which Christ is both the foundation and the Chief Cornerstone.[13] *This* is "the Word of God spread". *This* is the discipling of the nations. *This* is the Great Commission. This is the picture of Jesus with his own disciples. Laying such foundations however demands time—in fact, it demands full-time, full-energy labor. The Levites were, in their calling, set apart to give the time that was necessary to be keepers of knowledge, keepers of the altar, and keepers of the temple.

---

[7] Ephesians 4:11, 2:19-22; 1 Corinthians 3:10

[8] 1 Corinthians 3:9,16; Ephesians 2:21

[9] John 6:63

[10] Acts 5:20

[11] 1 Corinthians 3:11

[12] Galatians 3:13-14 – "*Christ redeemed us from the curse of the law by becoming a curse for us--for it is written, "Cursed is everyone who is hanged on a tree"-- so that in Christ Jesus the blessing of Abraham might come to the Gentiles, so that we might receive the promised Spirit through faith.*"

[13] Ephesians 2:20

Today, God's church still demands the same kind of energy and time of individuals specially called to the work of spreading the Word of God. Paul illustrates this clearly in 1 Corinthians 9:9-14:

For it is written in the Law of Moses, "You shall not muzzle an ox when it treads out the grain." Is it for oxen that God is concerned? Does he not speak entirely for our sake? It was written for our sake, because the plowman should plow in hope and the thresher thresh in hope of sharing in the crop. If we have sown spiritual things among you, is it too much if we reap material things from you? If others share this rightful claim on you, do not we even more? Nevertheless, we have not made use of this right, but we endure anything rather than put an obstacle in the way of the gospel of Christ. Do you not know that those who are employed in the temple service get their food from the temple, and those who serve at the altar share in the sacrificial offerings? In the same way, the Lord commanded that those who proclaim the gospel should get their living by the gospel.

These are people entrusted with the stewardship of preaching the gospel vocationally, such as were the other apostles, the brothers of the Lord, and Peter.[14] However, some may choose to preach the gospel of their own will under a special leading and strengthening of the Holy Spirit without taking money just as Paul and Barnabas did. They may forsake the right to get married or eat and drink well and choose to live frugally and work odd jobs or side jobs to sustain themselves so as to maintain their

---

[14] 1 Corinthians 9:17

ground for boasting for the sake of the Gospel as they give their lives to preaching it. They choose to serve as soldiers at their own expense.[15] In such cases they have a reward for their labors. Both of these are equally called and equally needed in the Church body, but it is those apostolic missionaries who wish to refrain from marrying and refrain from working for a living[16] to preach the Gospel where Christ has not been named that deserve our special attention and support.

BEING A MISSIONARY

There is no underlying agenda or hidden greed for gain in the ambassador for Christ. He simply aims to pour forth and pass on the love of the Father to a dying world. One of the great maldevelopments in modern missions and evangelism is the mixing of gospel with individualism which has made it about *the people*. It is not about the people. Spreading the gospel is about the Lord Jesus Christ. Christ sends us to a place, a people, a street corner, or an individual, for *his* sake, not theirs. The people are not our problem or our burden, they are Christ's burden. Our burden is the light and easy yoke of Jesus, not the problems of mankind. To go for the sake of man is to get things twisted around backwards and to invite burnout and disappointment in little to no time.

In today's world reaching the unreached is a crooked and tricky path to head down, but it is not impossible—nothing is impossible to him who believes. You must only pursue the

---

[15] 1 Corinthians 9:7
[16] I Corinthians 9:6

heavenly calling by and through the Holy Spirit. All callings are to be brought into submission to the one great calling which is upward and straight into the Holy of Holies. Paul writes it clearly: "I press on toward the goal for the prize of the *upward* call of God in Christ Jesus."[17]

It is important to think about the complex web of global affairs of our day and their implications on the gospel. Restriction and opposition are much greater than they used to be. Nationalism and civil wars are everywhere plunging nations into great identity crises. The Jesus-way therefore becomes an infringement on an already volatile situation if it is not presented in a right and loving way. The gospel must be put on display[18], whether with words or otherwise, but not crudely proselytized. Jesus taught his students to evangelize as he did and Jesus never smacked anybody around with the gospel, save the hypocrites. Often he pushed away crowds, or tried to avoid them. In the Muslim context and under the Islamic worldview, Christianity is an earthly kingdom. They do not see it as a kingdom "not of this world." The immediate problem that one runs into in the Islamic world then, is one of a clash of world kingdoms. Therefore, care must be taken to bypass this worldview to bring the gospel in a manner worthy of what it is, and not as a political or social regime.

A "proselyte" in the New Testament was one who was converted to Judaism. Consider the following words of Jesus in a Christian evangelistic context: "Woe to you, scribes and Pharisees [false interpreters and legalists], hypocrites! [fakes!] For you travel across sea and land to make a single proselyte [convert], and when

---

[17] Philippians 3:14 (Emphasis added)
[18] Matthew 5:16

he becomes a proselyte [convert], you make him twice as much a child of hell as yourselves!"[19]

Why would the proselytism of the 'false interpreters' and 'legalists', who traveled across the seas and lands to bring converts into Judaism, create people more wicked than they were? Perhaps, in a sense, they sow the wind and they reap the whirlwind.[20] They bear fruit from their own seed, each according to its kind on the earth.[21] This situation has long been part-and-parcel of Christianity, even since the beginning, producing many, many oppressive and imposing "Christians" throughout the ages, but more so today since it was said that such wickedness would increase.[22] Outsiders, agnostics, atheists, the Left (and increasingly the Right), Stoics, and Epicureans alike are more than sick and tired of the composure of such so-called Christians. So let's not imitate these so-called Christians' pomp and show, but rather seek to imitate good. Whoever does good is from God; whoever does evil has not seen God.[23] The U.N. International Covenant on Civil and Political Rights says this in Article 18:

> 1. Everyone shall have the right to freedom of thought, conscience and religion. This right shall include freedom to have or to adopt a religion or belief of his choice, and freedom, either individually or in community with others and in public or private, to manifest his religion or belief in worship, observance, practice and teaching.
> 2. No one shall be subject to coercion which would impair his freedom to have or to adopt a religion or belief of his choice.
> 3. Freedom to manifest one's religion or beliefs may be subject only

---

[19] Matthew 23:15
[20] Hosea 8:7
[21] Genesis 1:11
[22] Matthew 24:12
[23] 3 John 1:11

to such limitations as are prescribed by law and are necessary to protect public safety, order, health, or morals or the fundamental rights and freedoms of others.

4. The States Parties to the present Covenant undertake to have respect for the liberty of parents and, when applicable, legal guardians to ensure the religious and moral education of their children in conformity with their own convictions.[24]

This is a good example showing a world tired of the proselytism. The most effective time-tested methods in the realm of missions are non-tactical, non-confrontational and non-interfering means that are natural such as running businesses, being in the medical field, teaching English or other subjects, piloting, hospitality, and even just being a family sold out for God.[25] We need more conversation and proclamation, and less confrontation. When the body of Christ re-learns the art of conversation and proclamation combined with prayer and intercession, only then will we see the power of God working beyond anything we can ask, do, or think.

There is a place for stark confrontation however. The examples of hard, piercing confrontation and preaching in the New Testament are those of God's servants confronting people who knew the truth and who even acknowledged it with their lips, but whose hearts were far from Him. They were a stubborn and stiff necked people. You will not likely find this kind of situation among the unreached of the world.

---

[24] The U.N. International Covenant on Civil and Political Rights. Article 18. http://www.ohchr.org/english/law/ccpr.htm

[25] Joshua 24:15

CONTEXTUALIZED "GOING"

Most of the Church has run into this problem at one time or another. The world around us is changing, but the Church is not. The consequence is a growing disconnection that has spanned a good century after the Church began to lose its influence in our society. Today there is a great shaking of the Church as it reels and careens between a multitude of ideas involving the question of whether to contextualize or to stick with traditions. This kind of shaking or tension has actually been a common struggle time and time again since the beginning of Church. Debates and heated discussions rise and fall with every passing cultural shift. From the radical changes in the time of Paul and Peter, the Nicene Fathers, Augustine, Boniface, John of Damascus, Luther, Wesley, and so on, the Church has faced the same question we face to today. How do we go into our world?

The Church must not contextualize its "being". It must contextualize its "going". We are first chosen out of the world and set apart from the world, and we know that anyone who makes himself a friend of the world makes himself an enemy of God. The world and God are at total odds with each other. We must *be* on God's side in all circumstances and in all situations. There is no room for compromise on this. At the same time, we must *go* into the enemy's territory to fight against darkness and to plunder it of all its enslaved souls. This requires the utmost contextualization and strategy to reach every corner with the gospel. We must have the proper weapons, skill, and tact to penetrate the enemy's forces. Satan is not as prone to stupidity as some would think, but presents a very real challenge to the spread of God's glory and therefore we must be tactile, not ignorant of his devices. We bring the gospel to lost souls on their terms whatever they may be, and to wherever they may be. The message of the gospel however, is to come out and be free. It is just like Moses going into Egypt with a specific plan, and then leading them *out*. To remain with them in Egypt would not do; they had to separate themselves and go from there. The world will chase us down to try to recapture us just as the Egyptians did the Israelites, but this should press us to seek God all the more for his help to carry on. Yet, many give up and even rebel only to become slaves once again to the world. The church that caves in and goes back to the world is no less cowardly than the Israelites when they complained, "Let us choose a leader and go back to Egypt!"[26] The Church is not meant to *be* like Egypt. It is meant to *go* to Egypt and *bring out* the lost from Egypt. The contextualization is in the *going* and the *bringing out*.

WESTERNIZED MISSIONS

As Christianity continues to mature, we find ourselves entering an age of missions focused on the spread of the gospel in a non-ethnocentric manner. A lot of the history of missions has shown itself to be a spread of the gospel with colonial westernization attached to it. Far too many cultures and indigenous people groups have been stripped of their identities in music, dance, art, and communication styles, only to be replaced by Western forms of music, art, and communication styles. Dancing was considered "pagan", "satanic", or otherwise unacceptable for believers. But who said the Western forms were

---

[26] Numbers 14:4

the right ones? Wolfgang Simson writes:

> Although there are approximately 240 nations in the world, the last few centuries have seen great activity in just four countries in exporting their models of church into all the world: Germany, the UK, the USA, and Italy...While I do not at all deny the blessings of this mission era, it has also led to one of the greatest monopolizations of church around the world, where one western model of church has become a standard and dominating practice almost everywhere. American writer Gene Edwards decries this in the title of this disturbing book 'The Americanization of the Church' and we need to remind ourselves of the simple fact that Jesus was not a 'Westerner'. Given the fact that the four main missionary-world powers have been caught up in world wars against each other, killing each other in front of the eyes of the rest of the world, we need to realize that, as 'Christian nations', they lost a large amount of global Christian credibility. The West may have money, materials, rhetoric, and even a well-oiled mission machinery, but these cannot replace a genuine calling from God. I believe we have moved from a colonial era of mission into what I call 'national mission', where each nation is called to develop its own models of church. Often enough this will have to happen through people in every nation praying for themselves, shedding their own tears, incarnating the living Christ afresh within their own time and culture. If the West could then come and, in the spirit of 'crucified colonialism'---the opposite of imperialism and denominationalism---carefully pour some oil on this process, it would be wonderful.

The time has come for the Church to begin identifying its ethnocentric mistakes and making things right with minority groups and indigenous peoples who have been stripped of their God-given heritage. The Church needs to go beyond making apologies and begin embracing the art, dance, music, and communication styles of other cultures and allow these peoples to bring their cultural treasures to the feet of Jesus as sacrificial offerings of worship. Up until now, conformity has been the name of the game. Yet, the greatest testimony of the Church that is still to come will be a unity between peoples with a vast diversity of differences.

What About the Native Peoples?

"Pride and arrogance…I hate." – Wisdom, Proverbs 8:13

Let another praise you, and not your own mouth; a stranger, and not your own lips. Proverbs 27:2

We have heard of the pride of Moab— he is very proud— of his loftiness, his pride, and his arrogance, and the haughtiness of his heart. Jeremiah 48:29

Our Church has a root sin that continues to go unchecked and largely ignored. It is one thing and at the same time, many things. It is an injustice toward the First Nations peoples of this land who were grossly abused by greed and utilitarian religiosity. It is the later injustice of the slave trade and the gross maltreatment of Africans. It is the pride and arrogance of an ethnocentric white-man religion which sees itself as set apart and right in its cultural makeup. It is a hypocrisy that leads many leaders to "tie up heavy burdens, hard to bear, and lay them on people's shoulders".[1] It a sin that burns out countless numbers of followers and would-be followers. It is the sin of ethnocentrism— a subtle yet pervasive pride which exalts its own kind and identity over others. We thought we had a "manifest destiny" as white

---

[1] Matthew 23:4

people in a new land, yet God has laid out his manifest destiny for all mankind in Jesus Christ who came to end the sin of ethnocentrism and create peacemakers to bring healing around the world.

Because of our individualistic worldview most Americans have no understanding about how to identify with national sins, and rarely take any responsibility for them. But God sees and knows them, and he knows them well.[2] Nehemiah's example is a good model of what it means to step up and take responsibility for the sins of your nation. Richard Twiss explains,

> Nehemiah is a great study in praying with identification. Though Nehemiah had never lived in Jerusalem and did not personally contribute to its spiritual condition, he prayed, "Both my father's house and I have sinned" (Neh. 1:6). Like Nehemiah, we must identify with the wrongs of our country and own them as they relate to the oppression of Native peoples.[3]

He further notes, "I believe there is a prophetic call from the heart of God to the Anglo church in America to recognize its historical and continued racism and indifference toward its Native brethren—and to make amends."[4]

John Dawson writes:

> If we have broken our covenants with God and violated our relationships with one another, the path to reconciliation must begin with the act of confession. The greatest wounds in

---

[2] *Sinful nations and cities*, see Isaiah 1:4, Zephaniah 3
[3] Richard Twiss, One Church Many Tribes, p.171
[4] Ibid. p.49

human history, the greatest injustices, have not happened through the acts of some individual perpetrator, rather through the institutions, systems, philosophies, cultures, religions and governments of mankind. Because of this, we, as individuals, are tempted to absolve ourselves of all individual responsibility. Unless somebody identifies themselves with corporate entities, such as the nation of our citizenship, or the subculture of our ancestors, the act of honest confession will never take place. This leaves us in a world of injury and offense in which no corporate sin is ever acknowledged, reconciliation never begins and old hatreds deepen.

The followers of Jesus are to step into this impasse as agents of healing. Within our ranks are representatives of every category or humanity.[5]

The Church in America has been largely numb to the need for repentance and humility toward our Native brothers and sisters. Its potential is stifled because of this. Groups of Puritan settlers in various places took liberally of what did not belong to them in the name of "manifest destiny". At the same time they preached Jesus. They held to a legalist mindset that led them to act like the Israelites of the Old Testament routing out people whom they counted as "savages" and taking their land from them. The American Church is still deeply buried in this sin. Dawson continues,

It is obvious that modern America has inherited both blessings and curses as a legacy from the past, but we do not understand what has happened to us as clearly as Nehemiah did. We, too, sense both captivity and loss, but we have forgotten who we are. Americans have a deep yearning to be part of a healthy nation doing good in

---

[5] John Dawson, *Healing America's Wounds*, (Ventura: Regal Books, 1994), p.30

the world, yet we are drifting into the future without purpose and without hope.[6]

A simple survey of today's Church in America reveals beyond debate a deeply segmented and racially divided Church. John Perkins observed that the evangelical church is the most segregated, racist institution in America.[7] Historically, minority ethnic groups have gone to great ends to become like Christian white people, but very rarely have we white people made any effort to become like our other non-white brothers and sisters in spite of a clear biblical teaching about what it means to *share* in the blessing of the gospel:

To the weak I became weak, that I might win the weak. I have become all things to all people, that by all means I might save some. I do it all for the sake of the gospel, that I may share with them in its blessings. 1 Corinthians 9:22-23

Instead, we white people have laid heavy burdens, hard to bear, on the shoulders of peoples different from us, and we have held to a spirit of pride and arrogance that see these people and their cultures as less than and inferior to ours. It has often taken figures from among the oppressed people themselves to sacrifice their necks to speak out against the injustice and see things changed. Where are the prophets of the white people to speak out against the racism? This corporate testimony of our church is the very thing that the world mocks and sneers at. It is not a testimony of unity, but of division. It is not a testimony of the

---

[6] Ibid. p.50
[7] John M. Perkins, *With Justice for All*, (Ventura: Regal Books, 1982), p. 108

Kingdom of God which is made up of peoples from every tribe, ethnicity, and language, but a testimony of rivalry and division. It is not a testimony of love for one another, but enmity with one another.

There is a prayer of Jesus that stands out in light of this unholy struggle in our Church:

"I do not ask for these only, but also for those who will believe in me through their word, that they may all be one, just as you, Father, are in me, and I in you, that they also may be in us, so that the world may believe that you have sent me." John 17:20-21

Oh, that we may all be *one!* The white American Church must cease its ethnocentric activities and marketing strategies and learn to love its neighbor, and currently, our neighbors are suffering from marginalization, discrimination, poverty, and neglect from the larger Church. Large refugee communities have moved into the neighborhoods in the last decade, but churches have not embraced them or welcomed them. Did the Gospel fail to do what it was sent for? Certainly not. We as a Western Church have simply failed to preach the gospel, for the gospel is impartial, and teaches that the least will inherit the earth, that the least will enter the kingdom of God before us, and the least will be the greatest.[8] We have boasted in our own glories and praised ourselves for our intellect, prosperity, and mega-ministries while looking down upon the differences of the Native and African-American communities, and not only those communities but other ethnic groups as well. The African-American and Native American communities have been some of the most repressed

---

[8] Luke 7:28, 9:48; Matthew 5:5; Isaiah 29:19

people in the world and our lack of relationship and partnership with them in the gospel is a constant rebuke to our faces.

Simply, we need to get our hands off them and let them be free to be God's own offspring and not our offspring. This means reconciliation and giving them back their lives, their culture, and their heritage. This means honoring them as those who will enter the Kingdom of God before us. It is not enough to say to say apologies and wish them well. Dawson adds, "I believe there is to be much more than reconciliation and peaceful coexistence with justice. I believe there is to be a flowering of Indian decorative arts, language, culture and dance that is championed by the Church."[9] We must not love in word or talk, but in action and truth. If we can't do that, how does God's love abide in us?[10]

---

[9] John Dawson, *Healing America's Wounds*, (Ventura: Regal Books, 1994), pp.178-179
[10] 1 John 3:16-18

Men and Women

The wounds inflicted by men and women on each other constitute the fundamental fault line running beneath all other human conflict. If gender difference is used as the justification for the devaluation of one part of humanity, then the door is opened for the selective devaluation of all of humanity based on some difference from a perceived ideal. Gender conflict…is the biggest reconciliation issue of all, outside of our need to be reconciled to God the Father. John Dawson, Healing America's Wounds

Postmodern society would tell us simply, that men and women "happened", but under the biblical worldview we are given two distinct designs and purposes—one for our lower nature, and one for our heavenly nature. The difficulty we have in understanding this however, is not because the Bible isn't clear on what it says about manhood and womanhood, but because of our pride and the pure profoundness and mystery behind manhood and womanhood which many of us are ignorant of. There is a wealth of instruction about manhood and womanhood in the Bible yet it is not as easy to understand as a lot of other doctrines and many of us are divided over it. It may be a surprise to some, but it seems that the New Testament gives us a dualistic view of complimentarianism *and* egalitarianism.

*Neither was man created for woman, but woman for man…**nevertheless in the Lord** the woman is not independent of man nor man of the woman… 1 Corinthians 11:9,11*

The woman was originally created with a purpose to help the man but in Christ we are both equally dependent upon one another. Do you see the dialectic? We have a higher and a lower nature and they are not the same. John Wesley notes, "Nevertheless in the Lord Jesus, there is neither male nor female - neither is excluded; neither is preferred before the other in his kingdom."[1] At home spouses may be husband and wife, but at the same time in Christ's kingdom, they are brother and sister.

Likewise, husbands, live with your wives in an understanding way, showing honor to the woman as the weaker vessel, since they are heirs with you of the grace of life, so that your prayers may not be hindered. 1 Peter 3:7

Again, Peter says women, though weaker, are equal heirs in the grace of life. Therefore, show honor to them.

Sexism, racism, and discrimination are products of sin. The bible teaches us to love each other and that we are one through Christ without whom we are bound to sexist and racist attitudes. In the Holy Spirit we are re-created the same—there is neither male nor female—and in the Kingdom there won't be any marriage.[2] Yet, while we are now sons and daughters of God, we still walk around as sons and daughters of Adam and Eve in whom we are definitively male and female.[3] Women are equal to men as all were created equal, but we were not created the same originally. As far as our lower nature is concerned, strength is an authority in its own right. So the natural order of authority lies in the area of strength and weakness.

---

[1] John Wesley's Notes on the Entire Bible, 1765, 1 Corinthians 11:11
[2] Matthew 22:30, Galatians 3:28
[3] Genesis 1:27

"Ask the prior question, is sexuality anything more than biology?'"
"Masculinity means initiation…God is the initiator."
"Femininity means response. "[4]
- Elizabeth Elliot

When it comes to the problem of understanding the male from the female we have to think spiritually, and let the Spirit lead us into the truth.[5] Otherwise there could be something vital missing from our instruction if we don't have the spiritual eyes necessary because,

This mystery is profound, and I am saying that it refers to Christ and the church.[6]

Going to the beginning God shows us his intention for creating the male and female:

And God blessed them. And God said to them, "Be fruitful and multiply and fill the earth and subdue it and have dominion over the fish of the sea and over the birds of the heavens and over every living thing that moves on the earth.[7]

He created them male and female, and blessed them, and called their

---

[4] Elizabeth Elliot. *The Mark of a Man.* (Grand Rapids, MI: Fleming H. Revell, 1981).
[5] John 16:13
[6] *Ephesians 5:32*
[7] Genesis 1:28

name Adam in the day when they were created.[8]

ORIGINAL CREATION

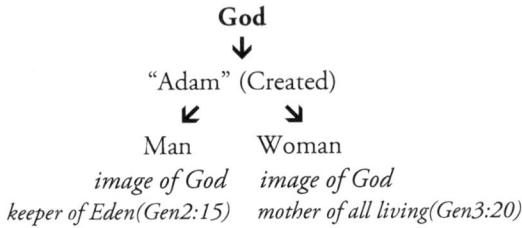

God
↓
"Adam" (Created)
↙ ↘
Man Woman
image of God *image of God*
keeper of Eden(Gen2:15) *mother of all living(Gen3:20)*

And the rib that the LORD God had taken from the man he made into a woman and brought her to the man. Then the man said, "This at last is bone of my bones and flesh of my flesh; she shall be called Woman [ishah], because she was taken out of Man [ish]." Therefore a man shall leave his father and his mother and hold fast to his wife, and they shall become one flesh.[9]

For not all flesh is the same, but there is one kind for humans, another for animals, another for birds, and another for fish.[10]

What is important to us here is the oneness intended between the man and woman as illustrated in these scriptures. They are a king and queen to be keepers of the earth together as one. They both are named one name by God: *Adam*. "Adam" was a formal

---

[8] Genesis 5:2
[9] Genesis 2:22-24
[10] 1 Corinthians 15:39

name given to Adam and Eve and to all of us by God.[11] We are "Adam" by name. We were then given distinct and definitive roles and purposes for our dwelling on earth. Adam was to guard and protect, and Eve was to mother all the living.

THE NEW CREATION AND KINGDOM OF GOD

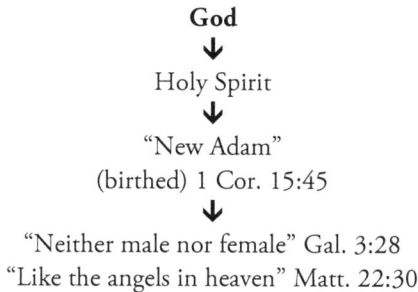

God
↓
Holy Spirit
↓
"New Adam"
(birthed) 1 Cor. 15:45
↓
"Neither male nor female" Gal. 3:28
"Like the angels in heaven" Matt. 22:30

Then a new thing happens for humanity through the grace of God: a plan to make all things new. God gives a new name to his people in Isaiah 62 which is a feminine name: "Hephzibah". This name means "my delight is in her". In essence, God renames us. In this Kingdom and new creation,

There is neither Jew nor Greek, there is neither slave nor free, there is no male and female, for you are all one in Christ Jesus.[12]

---

[11] A formal name in the Hebrew language was called "haShem" mean *the name* which is a word frequently used by Jews to refer to God.
[12] Galatians 3:28

For in the resurrection they neither marry nor are given in marriage, but are like angels in heaven.[13]

From now on, therefore, we regard no one according to the flesh. Even though we once regarded Christ according to the flesh, we regard him thus no longer. Therefore, if anyone is in Christ, he is a new creation. The old has passed away; behold, the new has come.[14]

Clearly, there is a lot of mystery and profoundness in this dualism. In the Kingdom of God we all have a new and different birth and are considered new creations. While we are no longer to regard people according to the flesh anymore we must still submit to the order of the original creation as long as we are in it.[15] Why? Because there is an original design and "wiring" which must still be followed to keep present families and social structures—including the local church—strong and flowing. Otherwise things tend to fall apart and become a dysfunctional mess as we are currently witnessing in our times. So it is not a matter of following rules or the law because we are not under those; it is a matter of *design*.

---

[13] Matthew 22:30

[14] 2 Corinthians 5:16-17

[15] In Ephesians 6:1-4 Paul teaches submission according to the order of the original creation in the context of parents and children even though in the Kingdom of God they are not parents and children but siblings: *Children, obey your parents in the Lord, for this is right. "Honor your father and mother" (this is the first commandment with a promise), "that it may go well with you and that you may live long in the land." Fathers, do not provoke your children to anger, but bring them up in the discipline and instruction of the Lord."* The same would hold true in the order of husbands and wives.

***

We live and walk according to the Spirit as a holy nation. We are the Kingdom of God witnessing its reality and coming fulfillment to the world. As it is, we have two natures which come from two totally different places. The tension between the two is great but we must always remember where our true allegiance and hope is. Our old nature must be a slave to our new nature and not the other way around. In the following passage in Ephesians, Paul speaks dialectically of how our new nature and relationship with each other and toward Christ relates to how we ought to be in our original nature within marriage.

Wives, submit to your own husbands, as to the Lord. For the husband is the head of the wife even as Christ is the head of the church, his body, and is himself its Savior. Now as the church submits to Christ, so also wives should submit in everything to their husbands. Husbands, love your wives, as Christ loved the church and gave himself up for her, that he might sanctify her, having cleansed her by the washing of water with the word, so that he might present the church to himself in splendor, without spot or wrinkle or any such thing, that she might be holy and without blemish. In the same way husbands should love their wives as their own bodies. He who loves his wife loves himself. For no one ever hated his own flesh, but nourishes and cherishes it, just as Christ does the church, because we are members of his body. "Therefore a man shall leave his father and mother and hold fast to his wife, and the two shall become one flesh." This mystery is profound, and I am saying that it refers to Christ and the church. However, let each one of you love his wife as himself, and let the wife see that she respects her husband. [16]

The all important role of headship is seen throughout these scriptures in the form of love. According to God's purpose in his creation, the one who is the head, or source, becomes the one who loves and lays down his life for the off-spring. That is because they love and treasure them above all else. To scorn it as a master-slave idea is incorrect because the master is not going to have any interest in laying down his life for his slave. That is often an ignorant modern-day accusation against the off-spring relationships throughout God's creation. It is something that is not only evident in the world of humans, but throughout the animal kingdom as well. Oh how we need to see men laying down their lives for their wives and families again! At the same time in the Kingdom of God, we find ourselves under a different mode of being where we are all equally to submit to one another as brothers and sisters because Christ is now the "head of the household".

Therefore equality is not about our value or roles or desires. Equality is about God's love. We all have inequalities—all sorts of them. But what sort of people ought we to be in regards to these inequalities? Firstly, we must be like God, who is no respecter of persons and who shows no partiality. Secondly, we have to be obedient to his will for our design as humans, for this pleases God.

---

[16] Ephesians 5:22-33

The Authority of the Word cannot be Broken

...Scripture cannot be broken. John 10:35

Over the centuries in Western civilization, the Bible has consistently sustained a position of undisputed authority and sacredness. Figures such as Augustine, Thomas Aquinas, and the Reformers, have afforded the Church a sense of stability and permanence as it held a position of authority and influence within society as the entrusted bearer of the Holy Scriptures.[1] Yet within the last century the Church has dramatically lost its influential and authoritative witness in society, and its sense of stability has grown less and less.

Today, through the many scientific advances, denominational splits, and all the theological hairsplitting, the Bible has come under the lens of scrutiny and its validity as the binding testimony of God upon humanity has been profoundly challenged. Now, it seems as though Christianity's authoritative witness is more questionable than ever. So the question is, in light of the postmodern shifts in our society and the subsequent marginalization of the Church, does the Bible still retain a binding authority from God upon humanity? To answer that question we should seek to understand it in conjunction with the role of the Church and the Holy Spirit in the world.

---

[1] Erickson, M. 1987. *Christian Theology*, 59-60. Michigan: Baker Book House

This stand-point of authority is heavily challenged by postmodernism. We'll employ a philosophical sense of postmodernism where there have been shifts in thinking through philosophical figures such as Hegel, Nietzsche, Freud, Sartre, and the like. Ultimately this shift in thinking has led in a direction toward the belief that the nature of a human being is no different than the nature of any other animal. This materialistic worldview has consequently given rise to the attitudes that truth is relative, or within you, or constantly changing. Nietzsche asserts,

> What then is truth? A movable host of metaphors, metonymies, and anthropomorphisms: in short, a sum of human relations which have been poetically and rhetorically intensified, transferred, and embellished, and which, after long usage, seem to a people to be fixed, canonical and binding.[2]

The postmodern attack on the Bible is that it is really nothing more than a creation of a highly advanced and complex animal. One of the prominent results of the postmodern shift is a reductionist approach to knowledge and worldview. The Interdisciplinary Encyclopedia of Religion and Science states:

> A reductionist believes that a complex system is nothing but the sum of its parts. An account of it can be reduced to accounts of individual constituents. An antireductionist believes that the whole

---

[2] Nietzsche, F. 1979. "On Truth and Lies in a Nonmoral Sense" in Philosophy and Truth: Selections from Nietzsche's Notebooks of the early 1870's, p. 84. New Jersey: Humanities Press International

is more than the sum of its parts. There are holistic properties that cannot be described in purely constituent terms.[3]

What does not happen in a reductionist worldview however, is the discovery of holistic truth and knowledge. What is holistic truth and knowledge? It is separate and distinct from a mere collection of facts. It is the very design of those facts. It is the software not made possible by binary code, but by intelligent design using that code. It is the story or poem not made possible by collecting words and letters, but by an inspired creativity using those words and letters. It is the human being, not made possible by the chance happening of many genes pooling together, but by the design of a Creator using those genes. The reductionist has his back turned toward the meaning of every bit of empirical data he comes across and, in effect, sees no meaning or holistic truth. For Nietzsche, truth was merely a collection of facts that have been designated by common tradition as such. But if you are focused only on the data, you will never see the program. George MacDonald helps us to see in a very practical way through something as simple as a flower how truth is separate from facts or a collection of facts. Approaching a flower in a postmodern, reductionist way, one can reduce it to pedals, pollen, and a stalk. He then can reduce each of those components to an indefinite number of micro-components until—to him—the flower becomes nothing more than molecules and atoms. MacDonald writes, "Ask a man of mere science what is the truth of the flower. He will pull it to pieces, show you its parts, explain how they

---

[3] Tanzella-Nitti G., Larrey P. and Strumia A. "Reductionism". Interdisciplinary Encyclopedia of Religion and Science. http://www.disf.org/en/Voci/104.asp (accessed January 21, 2009)

operate, how they each contribute to the life of the flower…"[4]
Yet this yields only facts, and not a holistic truth, and therefore
does nothing to answer the question. Answering the question of
the truth of the flower then, forces us to go the opposite
direction. This compels us to think about it in a way that is still
empirically observable but is holistic rather than reductive. What
you are looking for, you will find. If you look for nothing else but
facts, that's exactly what you'll find. MacDonald writes:

> The truth of the flower is not the facts about it, be they correct as
> ideal science itself can discern them, but the shining, glowing,
> gladdening, patient thing enthroned on its stalk—the compeller of
> smiles and tears from child and prophet…The idea of God is the
> flower. His idea is not the botany of the flower. Its botany is but a
> thing of ways and means—of canvas and colour and brush in
> relation to the picture in the painter's brain…The mere intellect
> can never discover that which owes its being to the heart supreme.[5]

Thus we arrive at the postmodern issue with the Bible.
Through reductionism, the Bible is broken down into smaller,
apparently insignificant pieces until the reductionist can
satisfactorily say, "See, it's just a matter of pieces of paper, ink,
and the processes of the biogenic amines of someone's brain, and
therefore it has no authority over me." Albert Mohler describes
postmodern reductive thinking as a direct challenge even to the
gospel itself in that it undermines all "metanarratives" holding

---

[4] MacDonald, G. The Truth in Jesus. Edited by Michael Phillips.
(Minneapolis, MN: Bethany House, 2006). p.20
[5] Ibid. pp.21-22

them as oppressive or totalitarian and the gospel is most assuredly a metanarrative.[6]

As we have seen through the observations of George MacDonald, truths are not the same as facts. If we will see and understand the Bible as truth, we cannot break it down into an endless list of factual parts, no matter how correctly modern science may be able to discern them. Rather, it must be discovered as the word, that is, the holistic truth of Scripture—the redemptive, restoring, healing, powerful, life-preserving message straight from the mouth of God; the compeller of forgiveness, reconciliation, peace, love, goodness, joy, long-suffering, honor, faithfulness, mercy, etc. Such truths can even be empirically observed. The idea of God here is precisely what it ultimately speaks—*the word*—just as the idea of the flower is precisely the *flower*. His idea is not for the constituents of the word. Like God's design of the flower, the Bible's constituents are but things of ways and means—through many men, in many different times, in many different circumstances, and many different languages, various cultures and backgrounds, all of which work together to complete the ultimate message. It is a painting "of canvas and color and brush in relation to the picture in the painter's brain." We read in Psalm 119:160, "the sum of your word is truth", and in Galatians 5:14, "The whole law is fulfilled in one word: You shall love your neighbor as yourself."

As Paul describes a sentence as "one word" we are subsequently enlightened to the early Christians' understanding of the word of which they, and even Jesus himself, so often

---

[6] Mohler, A. He is Not Silent: Preaching in a Postmodern World. (Chicago, IL: Moody Publishers, 2008). p.118

spoke.[7] The apostle John states in the beginning of his gospel that Jesus was a living manifestation of that word. It is one that is an eternal, transcendent truth. Hence in John 14, Jesus spoke of himself as being the truth and not speaking anything save the word given to him from the Father.

Finally, if we will understand the proper role of the authority of the Bible in private and public spheres of life, it cannot be confused with enforcement. A common misunderstanding is that because the Bible is the authoritative Word of God given to the Church, we must therefore enforce its dictates on the world. This has been a strong and recurrent deception in the Church throughout its history—from the totalitarian Catholicism of the medieval era to the early days of the American Puritans—right into our own times with off-shoot evangelical movements of Christian nationalism and Christian Reconstructionism which say that Christians are called to rule the world. A journalist complains that some advocates of these ideologies "put dominionism—the idea that Christians have a God-given right to rule—at the center of the movement to bring evangelicals into politics."[8] The journalist goes on to explain that "dominionism is derived from a theocratic sect called Christian Reconstructionism, which advocates replacing American civil law with Old Testament biblical law."[9]

America's Church has become well known for its infamous capacity to enforce rules and cast shadows of condescension upon

---

[7] For example, Luke 8:11, 1 Joh 1:14, Acts 6:4, 19:20, Rom 10:8, 1 Co 1:18, Eph 6:17, Col 1:5, 2 Tim 2:9, 2:15, Tit 2:5, Heb 4:12, 11:3, Jas 1:22, 1 Pet 1:25, 2:8, 1 Joh 2:14, Rev 6:9, 20:4

[8] Goldberg, M. *Kingdom Coming: The Rise of Christian Nationalism.* (New York, NY: W.W. Norton & Company, 2007). p.13

[9] Ibid.

sinners. But the Bible is not the Church's gavel. It is the light to Church's path as it treads through darkness to its ultimate destination bringing with it all who will come to the light. It is the truth which sets people free. The Church is not meant to rule public life. It is meant to be a light and bring a blessing to all nations—the Son of God, Jesus Christ—as Galatians 3:14 clearly states. The early Christians understood this, and as Paul taught, The Scriptures were to be used for our profit and benefit towards good doctrine, correction, and instruction in the ways of righteousness. It was never meant to be used for worldly dictates or the enforcement of rules, outside the time of the nation of Israel.[10] The Greek word he uses is ὠφέλιμος which can be translated helpful, serviceable, or advantageous. It invokes a sense that we are given a treasure to help us along the way and that in Christ the Bible is for us rather than against us, that is, man is not for the Bible, but the Bible is for man. The world on the other hand, is condemned already. Is there any sense in both enforcing on people that which condemns them and preaching the gospel which forgives them at the same time? I think not.

The fulfillment of authority seems, according to scripture, to lie in a harmony between the Bible, the entire Church from beginning to end, and the Holy Spirit. This is because the Bible is considered the word of truth,[11] the Church is considered the temple of God and the pillar and buttress of truth,[12] and the Holy Spirit is considered the spirit of truth.[13] If then, the Church is to maintain an authoritative presence in the world it must

---

[10] 2 Timothy 3:16
[11] 2 Timothy 2:15
[12] 1 Timothy 3:15
[13] John 14:17, 15:26, 16:13

compel men by *doing truth* rather than by enforcing it or dictating it.

A reductive view of the Bible will lead one nowhere but to a nearly infinite number of facts, and away from the design. While language, books, people, and church congregations may be far from perfect, God shows himself in complete control by choosing to use such things for revealing perfect truth. This can be observed in a holistic way. Christ's incarnation was into imperfect flesh like ours susceptible to temptation, pain, bleeding, and death. Yet, he held complete control and was without sin. When we take a holistic stance toward truth we will see the authority of the Bible in a clear, glowing light as part of a profound unity with the Church and the Holy Spirit who indwells us.

What About the Broken Soul?

Many places to find a name
But this darkness won't let me go
Everyday is the same old game
Why can't I just let it flow?

Songs of love and butterflies
All I want is not there to have
Many words cast to and fro
But what about the broken soul?

Daunting tasks in the cold
Haunting masks in the fold
Treasures fill the air untold
When will come this light to mold?
Bound or free of letters' hold
Gasp and kick until its sold
Instant fire so I'm told

Just show me the simple tree
of love and life and why I'm free
Only give me a tiny seed
my greatest wish, desire, and need.

12 Reproofs for the Church

1. We must let the Spirit lead.

The wind blows where it wishes, and you hear its sound, but you do not know where it comes from or where it goes. So it is with everyone who is born of the Spirit. John 3:8

It is truer than ever that many are turned off and disheartened by the institutionalized or politicized scene so prevalent in our mainline churches. They are all too often cut and dry, over-organized, or just plain dead because they are more man-centered than Christ-centered. We have become so bound to a multitude of pressures and obligations that we lead, and pray to God that the Spirit would follow us. This is a very typical picture of the contemporary our church where, sadly, many people are burning out and finding themselves disillusioned. Their faith is undercut, and their tongues are parched, and they wander like sheep without a shepherd.

The present "reformation" around the world however is seeing a reversal; a turning of what has long been upside down back to right side up. Our church must rediscover its roots in the *oikos* fellowship, the *familia dei*, rather than in a faceless crowd. God is all about family relationships in his Church, even as the Godhead is a family, but the age of mass media is radically isolating people from one another and therefore things need to change:

> According to him [Theo Sorg, former bishop of Württemberg], the church of the future can no longer afford to be a large administrative institution primarily providing social services and performing baptisms, weddings, and funerals. "We need to become a church of small house churches, of involved, committed groups, a church with attractive worship services and missional events and activities, a church in which spiritually sensitive individuals make themselves available to others, a church in which opportunities for connecting, personal conversations, and dialogue are being offered, a church in which the gospel of Jesus Christ can manifest its invitational character.
>
> …
>
> More often than not the private houses of individual members of the congregation represent an effective, low-cost missional-strategic solution. They are highly flexible and can be used as meeting places for worship and instruction as well as for missional proclamation, for evangelistic discussion groups, and for individual counseling— all in the personal context of the family…Worship and fellowship are thus solidly anchored in the everyday life of the congregation. Because Christian church members meet where they and others also live out their daily lives, entering the church does not involve entering (what is perhaps perceived to be) uniquely sacred space. As a result of the absence of this physical hurdle, an outsider is not as likely to be so hesitant in attending the worship service.[1]

The church that follows the leading of the Spirit is one that is alive. It does not merely survive. It flourishes. It is one that begins

---

[1] Gehring, Roger W. *House Church and Mission: The Importance of Household Structures in Early Christianity*. Peabody, Massachusetts: Hendrickson Publishers, 2004. pp.310-311

with families, not with faceless crowds. It stands upon the Holy Scriptures, and serves by the Spirit. No longer does man set the stage, but the Spirit does. He says, we do. He goes, we follow. He works, we receive. John Wesley comments on Romans 7:6 saying we are "dead to that whereby we were held - To our old husband, the law. That we might serve in newness of spirit - In a new, spiritual manner. And not in the oldness of the letter - Not in a bare literal, external way, as we did before."

Christ said, "I will build my church, and the gates of hell will not prevail against it." (Mat. 16:18) We are hard pressed to find these words true of most churches today as the majority are shrinking and dying. We need to rediscover the real church–where the gates of hell are powerless.

This is not radical. This is obedience. It is neither hard nor burdensome. It is God's own work: Christ will build his church and make it grow too.[2]

If we live by the Spirit, let us also walk by the Spirit. Galatians 5:25

For while we were living in the flesh, our sinful passions, aroused by the law, were at work in our members to bear fruit for death. But now we are released from the law, having died to that which held us captive, so that we serve in the new way of the Spirit and not in the old way of the written code. Romans 7:5-6

2. We must be fervent in the Spirit.

...fan into flame the gift of God. 2 Timothy 1:6

---

[2] 1 Corinthians 3:7

Fire shall be kept burning on the altar continually; it shall not go out. Leviticus 6:13

It is a wonder how much our Church lacks power against what is obviously a very powerful and influential society and culture in the Western world. Even with the most gifted preachers or creative talent it still seems to be sagging and lagging and overall, dying. We can't seem to even maintain our presence. You have likely heard in many places about the need for the Church to "rethink itself", or "be relevant" or "get on the forefront" of things. It is a prevalent theme everywhere you go these days.

Our Church has a legacy of doing many great things (as well as bad) in history. It also has a legacy for being misrepresented by counterfeit Christs and counterfeit teachings. At this point it is almost as if the Church is buried beneath layers of bad fortune, disillusionment, and retribution from a world that has a different kind of attitude toward the Church than what we might have expected: indifference. Of course that attitude is not globally universal. In some places our Body is referred to as "infidels" or "anti-revolutionary".

Here is what we should feel impressed about in our own nation: Our Church has been fighting fire with candlesticks, when we need to be fighting fire with fire. Consider the amount of life sucked up by arbitrary and trivial things like the Internet, TV, video games, and radio. America has about 750 televisions per capita (1000 people) and they sap 12+ hours per week out of people. Nearly everyone uses the internet, and for about 17 hours per week at that. But lets talk about Church for a moment. How much time is given to Church—simple and plain fellowship, prayer, the Word, and breaking bread every week? If we are real and honest with ourselves, we can say it is probably but a sliver of our time compared to the rest of the time-vacuums we are enslaved to. And there are Christians who *still* complain about it! So we play a few songs, remove time for prayer, and give them the 15 or 20 minute sermon that they want—get 'em in and get 'em out. It is probably not a stretch to say that the average Christian spends almost no time each week in authentic fellowship. And we are wimps because of it.

There is saying out in the world about America: "What do Americans do with all the time they 'save'?" Perhaps what we are talking about shows the answer: it's wasted. So in the onslaught of these consumers of peoples' time, our Church is responding with the drive-thru sermon. We are fighting fire with candlesticks.

So let's turn our minds onto a fiery church that can not only compete with these other fiery weapons, but *overcome* them. We'll revisit Acts chapter 2 wherein we find the description of just such a church. In this church they meet very plainly and with purpose. Forget the "how-to" brouhaha, and let's return to some roots: here they *devote* themselves to the Word, *and* prayer, *and* fellowship, *and* breaking bread. Who? Not the only the leaders, but *all*. And what's more, *day by day* they attended the temple *and* gathered in their homes!

Someone might say, "But they could afford to spend more time fellowshipping like that, and surely God doesn't require we make Church a daily practice!" But to that it must be asked, "And how many hours per week do you spend in front of the Internet or TV?" And what did God feel himself about this daily church fellowship going on? He *loved* it. In fact, it pleased him so much that "the Lord added to their number *day by day* those who were being saved." We would probably consider an episode like this to be a revival. I think for this old-school on-fire Christianity it was simply normal.

We'd like to see a church like this that could meet throughout the week, devoting themselves to prayer, the Word, fellowship, outreach, and meals. We'd like to see people throwing out the remotes and game consoles and clearing the tables to make room and time for the family, the brotherhood and the destitute if that what it takes. We'd like to see the old cliché of "Sunday morning church" fade into a by-word behind a robust and fiery, daily gathering of believers because it is otherwise simply *not* going to overcome anything in our society. It melts like flax in a heartbeat under the heat of every current trend and new technology, and then cowers into a cave, afraid to come out until it's seems safe to do so. And the thinking continues to float around that if we can just hone and sharpen that one or two hour service; if we just add one more program; if we can just make that one hour more impressive, more flashy, more captivating, more engaging, more lively, more dynamic, then we can have a chance! Far be it from us. We know no God who gives his people "a shot" or some mere chance. We know only one God, and he makes *conquerors*. What is the victory we have that overcomes the world? A one-hour faith amusement ride? Hardly. We are grossly underestimating our steadfastness and endurance, and it is costing us everything worked for in this country. We need Fire!

3. The Church is the people and can be anywhere.

The woman said to him, "Sir, I perceive that you are a prophet. Our fathers worshiped on this mountain, but you say that in Jerusalem is the place where people ought to worship." Jesus said to her, "Woman, believe me, the hour is coming when neither on this mountain nor in

Jerusalem will you worship the Father. You worship what you do not know; we worship what we know, for salvation is from the Jews. But the hour is coming, and is now here, when the true worshipers will worship the Father in spirit and truth, for the Father is seeking such people to worship him. God is spirit, and those who worship him must worship in spirit and truth. (John 4:16-24)

Three places of worship are brought up in this discussion between Jesus and the Samaritan woman. There was the spot on the hill where the Samaritans worshiped, the temple in Jerusalem where the Jews worshiped, and then a secret place within our hearts where true worshipers worship. Jesus said that the Father is looking for the third kind. Not only that, the temple and the hill are obsolete; they are not sacred. You are obligated to worship in the place of your heart. It is the *only* true worship. Those who will worship God the Father *must* worship in spirit and truth. A temple, chapel, or cathedral, etc., might be a place to find quietness or solitude, (or a lot of other things) but the idea that you need to go there to worship God is absurd for "the Most High does not dwell in houses made by hands, as the prophet says: 'Heaven is my throne, and the earth is my footstool. What kind of house will you build for me, says the Lord, or what is the place of my rest? Did not my hand make all these things?'" (Acts 7:48-50)

4. We must bring the Kingdom community to our homes but not forsake the assembly.

Jesus said to them, "Come and have breakfast." John 21:12

"The third kind of service should be a truly evangelical order and should not be held in a public place for allsorts of people. But those who want to be Christians in earnest and who profess the gospel with hand and mouth should sign their names and meet alone in a house somewhere to pray, to read, to baptize, to receive the sacraments, and to do other Christian work..." Martin Luther

To accomplish the Great Commission, we must disciple all the nations and peoples. But how is this done? Can we finish the task if we limit ourselves to large theaters and preaching? This was not Jesus' style of discipleship. Does that mean then, that Jesus has failed in building his church like he said he would?[3] Most certainly not.

Jesus is, in fact, building his church. But how? When we read the New Testament with open eyes, we can see those terms very clearly. For many centuries Christians have worked very hard in many ways in seeking the discipling of the nations. Very often however, it has been caught up in a dysfunctional mess of politics, greed, and personal agendas. Man is very capable of pouring lots of energy and resources into their agendas to make things work, but he cannot build the church no matter how hard he tries. So why are we pushing Jesus out of the picture and trying to take over his job? In a powerful picture painted by our brother Ezekiel, found in chapter sixteen of his book, we see a faithless Bride forsaking God and trying to do things on her own—and the result is a mess.

His salvation and his Holy Spirit have been made freely available to all. However his presence is conditional to the state that our hearts are in. The reality we must face is that though we

---

[3] Matthew 16:18

may gather together in a meeting house to hear a preacher and sing songs about God and see growing numbers of attendees and increased giving God may in fact not be moving and not be present—despite what many of us in the pulpits would like to believe. God can and does make us to succeed,4 but success does not mean that God is moving.5 Part of being sleepy, lukewarm Christians is growing numb enough to our desperate need of his Spirit to the point where we accept in a mechanical way that God is moving and present when in reality he's little more than omnipresent. Sin and disobedience to the gospel will hinder his manifest presence. Sacrifices and oblations do not automatically mean God shows up. God doesn't look for the tithe or the sacrifice of your time on Sunday morning or how hard you work on your sermon or how good your music is. He looks for the obedient heart. It is a faith-obedience and not a work-obedience.6 To obey is better than sacrifice!7 It is in this obedience that we find Christ moving and building his church.

The Gospel of the Kingdom needs our homes. Being a church means being a Kingdom family. Consequently, the simplest and most effective way of discipling nations is by planting families of the Holy Spirit. What is increasingly being called the "next reformation" is simply a movement of God to break the old status quo and flawed worldview that sees church chapels as sacred and houses as secular. It is not a voiding of local congregations by any means, but simply bringing balance back to a lopsided tradition. You will notice that when we read in Acts about the Christians

---

4 2 Chronicles 26:5, 1 Kings 2:3, 1 Samuel 18:14, Job 42:10-12
5 Isaiah 1:12-31, Revelation 3:14-20
6 Romans 1:5; 16:26
7 1 Samuel 15:22

gathering together, they gathered both on Solomon's Porch in great numbers and in houses as small close-knit families.

This is the pattern we see in the New Testament. Jesus reached out through the homes, taught in the homes, and trained his disciples to go from home to home to spread the gospel. The Church also started in the home, and disciples multiplied throughout the homes. Of course, these families also gathered together in the temple courts for preaching, strength, unity, and witness. But at the time of Constantine, this movement of the Holy Spirit was largely undermined when the ecclesiology of Church became less of a testament to a future Kingdom and more of an earthly political empire.

Consider the ways of worldly religion with the revolutionary Way that Jesus proclaimed with the coming of his Kingdom:

Religion:	The Way of Jesus:
Worship is sanctioned in temples; ritual and ceremony exclusive to temples.	Worship starts in your closet and consumes your entire lifestyle.[8]
Set-apart hours or days, places and objects; separation between "sacred" and "secular".	Set-apart lives (the Way of life); no division of "sacred" and "secular". All of creation is "sacred".[9]

---

[8] Matthew 6:6, Romans 12:1
[9] Psalm 24:1, 1 Corinthians 10:25-28

This Way of Jesus was destined to prosper on the household level of society. It does not undermine the place of vocational teachers and preachers of the word, nor does it undermine organization, structure, or liturgy. If anything, it *supports* those. There will always be organization, structure, and liturgy in our daily living as a family of God, small or large. This is because we are a fallen race in a fallen world. Yet, there is *freedom* in the Way of Jesus in all these things because it is ultimately the heart that God is after. Having a heart of worship the way Jesus described is humanly impossible just as the building of the Church is. We must worship in the Spirit and in Truth.[10] With man this is impossible, but with God all things are possible.

The church…multiplied. Acts 9:31
..the number of disciples multiplied greatly… Acts 6:7

5. We must reach the city.
You shall love your neighbor as yourself. Matthew 22:39

But seek the welfare of the city where I have sent you into exile, and pray to the Lord on its behalf, for in its welfare you will find your welfare. Jeremiah 29:7

There have always been cities—big, condensed, pliable containers of culture, neighbors, power, faith, and war. They harbor, they send out, they fortify, they spread out, they rise up, and they fall. They splurge, they protect, they seek, they isolate, and they multiply. Cities are the people. And the people are the

---

[10] Jeremiah 17:9, John 4:23-24, Luke 18:27

cities. E Pluribus Unum as the American coin says, or "From many, one". Cities are the indelible examples of how people unite, or don't unite, and what happens in the course thereafter. Cities have been around since the beginning. The ruins of many of the of old cities of the past remain to remind the future inhabitants that a city once existed here. They remind them that a force of many minds pooled together once drastically altered life and land long before they were even born. They were our fathers and mothers, and we came from them. We identify with them as people: we have culture because they had culture; we have customs because they had customs; we have intelligence because they had it first; and sadly, we have war because they had war. We are not separate from them nor are we different from them, but we were brought forth by them—we are of them. Sons of Man. Daughters of Man. In reality, there is no "tabula rasa".

In this vast "tree of life", as it were, no one could measure it's sheer overall size having grown from its roots of but one single family over the course of thousands of years. Yet it is relatively young: from the time of Noah there have only passed around 57 full 70-year generations. (Since 3-4 generations can be 'overlapping' at the same time, there have probably been at least a couple hundred generations total.) It is spectacular to realize the exponential growth from a couple parents to almost 7 billion children today in so few generations.

When the numbers grow, the cities grow, and they become powerful. In the story of the Tower of Babel about our ancient fathers and mothers we find an example of the capability of not only those people at that time, but of any people anywhere united in mass numbers together to do something 'great' for themselves. Cities today are nothing new, and the ambition to grow, be great, powerful, and wealthy, is nothing new either.

In the wisdom of the Proverbs we are given some guidelines for the differences between a blessed city and a cursed city. They are lessons to teach us not only how physical cities can benefit, but also how we, as citizens of the set-apart "City on a Hill", the Heavenly City of Jerusalem (Hebrew 12:22), can be blessed. Conversely, it shows us how we can end up as 'ancient ruins'. But it all depends on that 'blessing' upon which Proverbs 11:11 hinges. Therefore we pray for and seek the welfare of the city.

By the blessing of the upright a city is exalted, but by the mouth of the wicked it is overthrown. Proverbs 11:11

From out of the city the dying groan, and the soul of the wounded cries for help... Job 24:12

A wise man scales the city of the mighty and brings down the stronghold in which they trust. Proverbs 21:22

We need to be in the cities. More importantly, we need to be *wise* in the cities. In our age, money has become the church's evangelistic tool of choice. However, it has proved nothing. Too much money has been thrown scandalously into hasty and foolish ideas that have not been wrought in prayer or in waiting upon the Lord. The response to such church-foolery is city-mockery. The kind of witness that Jesus had on a city was starkly different—he would simply love his neighbor, and find suddenly that "the whole city was gathered together at the door."[11]

---

[11] Mark 1:29-34

What is the ultimate evangelistic tool? Here's what the LORD says:

When you reap the harvest of your land, you shall not reap your field right up to its edge, neither shall you gather the gleanings after your harvest. And you shall not strip your vineyard bare, neither shall you gather the fallen grapes of your vineyard. You shall leave them for the poor and for the sojourner: I am the Lord your God.

You shall not steal; you shall not deal falsely; you shall not lie to one another. You shall not swear by my name falsely, and so profane the name of your God: I am the Lord.

You shall not oppress your neighbor or rob him. The wages of a hired servant shall not remain with you all night until the morning. You shall not curse the deaf or put a stumbling block before the blind, but you shall fear your God: I am the Lord.

You shall do no injustice in court. You shall not be partial to the poor or defer to the great, but in righteousness shall you judge your neighbor. You shall not go around as a slanderer among your people, and you shall not stand up against the blood of your neighbor: I am the Lord.

You shall not hate your brother in your heart, but you shall reason frankly with your neighbor, lest you incur sin because of him. You shall not take vengeance or bear a grudge against the sons of your own people, *but you shall love your neighbor as yourself: I am the Lord.* [12]

---

[12] Leviticus 19:9-18

We are not to be partial to the poor, nor defer to the great. Instead God wants his people to be wise and to minister in love to those who fit the description of "neighbor". There is nothing very flashy or glamorous about this kind of witness, but it does show forth the great "I Am".

6. We cannot make ourselves Pastors.

If I glorify myself, my glory is nothing. John 8:54

The glory of a shepherd is not found in the study or the seminary, nor is it found in any self-produced skill or ability. Those who try to mold themselves into shepherds will only disillusion their sheep.

And I will give you shepherds after my own heart, who will feed you with knowledge and understanding. Jeremiah 3:15

Instead, shepherds are *given* not made. Reading from Ephesians 4:11, "He *gave* the apostles, the prophets, the evangelists, the shepherds and teachers." These roles are not born or bred of head knowledge, but from within the heart where the Spirit works. Because God provides these certain persons, it is distinct and certain when he does. One who is truly endowed with such giftings would recognize the inconceivable weight and glory of such an occupation and their utter inability to fulfill it apart from the risen Christ who declared, "you can do nothing apart from me." (John 15:5) He might actually be inclined to doubt and run from the idea just as Jonah ran from God's calling (Jonah 1:3), or as Moses doubted his calling (Exodus 3:11;

4:1,10, 13), or as Jeremiah was troubled by his calling (Jeremiah 1:6). Such a calling is a gift of the Spirit and thus provokes much wrestling with the Lord like Jacob did "for the desires of the flesh are against the Spirit, and the desires of the Spirit are against the flesh, for these are opposed to each other." (Galatians 5:17)

J. Oswald Chamber writes in his book *Spiritual Leadership,*

> Spiritual leaders are not elected, appointed, or created by synods or churchly assemblies. God alone makes them. One does not become a spiritual leader by merely filling an office, taking course work in the subject, or resolving in one's own will to do this task. A person must qualify to be a spiritual leader. (Chambers, p.18)

One can easily become a doctor, a pilot, an entrepreneur, or a professional of many sorts, but it is impossible for one to become a pastor, apostle, prophet, or teacher of the living God. They are only from the hand of God and as Jesus says, "with man it is impossible, but with God all things are possible."[13]

If one tries to make himself a shepherd (or a prophet, etc.) he deceives himself and his glory is nothing. What's worse is he sets up his flock for disaster and disillusionment, and in the end he will have to give account for his actions.

Jeremiah continues the prophecy...

For the shepherds are stupid and do not inquire of the Lord; therefore they have not prospered, and all their flock is scattered. Jeremiah 10:21

---

[13] Matthew 19:26

Many shepherds have destroyed my vineyard; they have trampled down my portion; they have made my pleasant portion a desolate wilderness. Jeremiah 12:10

Woe to the shepherds who destroy and scatter the sheep of my pasture! declares the Lord. Jeremiah 23:1

Therefore thus says the Lord, the God of Israel, concerning the shepherds who care for my people: "You have scattered my flock and have driven them away, and you have not attended to them. Behold, I will attend to you for your evil deeds, declares the Lord. Jeremiah 23:2

My people have been lost sheep. Their shepherds have led them astray, turning them away on the mountains. From mountain to hill they have gone. They have forgotten their fold. Jeremiah 50:6

And Ezekiel…

Son of man, prophesy against the shepherds of Israel; prophesy, and say to them, even to the shepherds, Thus says the Lord God: Ah, shepherds of Israel who have been feeding yourselves! Should not shepherds feed the sheep?" Ezekiel 34:2

As I live, declares the Lord God, surely because my sheep have become a prey, and my sheep have become food for all the wild beasts, since there was no shepherd, and because my shepherds have not searched for my sheep, but the shepherds have fed themselves, and have not fed my sheep… Ezekiel 34:8

And Zechariah too…

My anger is hot against the shepherds, and I will punish the leaders; for the Lord of hosts cares for his flock, the house of Judah, and will make them like his majestic steed in battle. Zechariah 10:3

In contrast to the shepherds after God's own heart…

I will set shepherds over them who will care for them, and they shall fear no more, nor be dismayed, neither shall any be missing, declares the Lord. Jeremiah 23:4

And I will give you shepherds after my own heart, who will feed you with knowledge and understanding. Jeremiah 3:15

7. We must protect our flocks.

Truly, truly, I say to you, he who does not enter the sheepfold by the door but climbs in by another way, that man is a thief and a robber. But he who enters by the door is the shepherd of the sheep. To him the gatekeeper opens. John 10:1-3

The environment of a sheepfold is a protected one in which the sheep are guarded from thieves, robbers, and wolves. The sheep know each other, and they know their shepherd. Jesus tells us that a good shepherd lays his life down for the sheep. The bad shepherds on the other hand, are the "hired hands" who "care nothing for the sheep." and "leaves the sheep and flees" when danger comes. (v.13) If the sheepfold is not protected by a good shepherd, the sheep will eventually be scattered. (v.12)

Therefore it becomes us as shepherds to know our flock and to know who is coming and going through the gate. This is the point of a "gatekeeper" (v.3). You don't just let anybody into the fold. We must, in fact, *beware* of dangerous figures or "false prophets, who come to you in sheep's clothing but inwardly are ravenous wolves." (Matthew 7:15)

And so the duty of a shepherd is crucial and must not be taken for granted…

Know well the condition of your flocks, and give attention to your herds… Proverbs 27:23

As a shepherd seeks out his flock when he is among his sheep that have been scattered… Ezekiel 34:12

Therefore the people wander like sheep; they are afflicted for lack of a shepherd. Zechariah 10:2

…seek the young…heal the maimed…nourish the healthy… Zechariah 11:16

Sometimes sheep need to be carried…

He will tend his flock like a shepherd; he will gather the lambs in his arms; he will carry them in his bosom, and gently lead those that are with young. Isaiah 40:11

He said to him a second time, "Simon, son of John, do you love me?" He said to him, "Yes, Lord; you know that I love you." He said to him, "Tend my sheep. John 21:16

8. We must not give to Caesar what doesn't belong to Caesar.

Render to Caesar the things that are Caesar's, and to God the things that are God's. Mark 12:17

The Church is a precious jewel, a royal diadem which belongs wholly to its builder, Christ. To give away the church, the bride, to the world, is truly adulterous and base. <u>Erastianism</u> is a concept from the 1500s introduced by a man named Thomas Erastus who believed that the state should reign supreme in church matters, and even take the role in punishing sins. But is not this betrayal and treason against a jealous God, Father, Husband, and King of Kings?

You adulterous people! Do you not know that friendship with the world is enmity with God? Therefore whoever wishes to be a friend of the world makes himself an enemy of God. (James 4:4-5)
… I the Lord your God am a jealous God… (Exodus 20:5)
No servant can serve two masters, for either he will hate the one and love the other, or he will be devoted to the one and despise the other. Matthew 6:24

The Church is a city on a hill devoted to shining a light in a land of darkness and providing a refuge for all who cry out Abba, Father. It does not cede its God-ordained mandate to worship to the discretion of the world, but worships, rather, in spite of it. How faithless it is to put it at the mercy of the world!

You also took your beautiful jewels of my gold and of my silver, which I had given you, and made for yourself images of men, and with them played the whore. And you took your embroidered garments to cover them, and set my oil and my incense before them. Also my bread that I gave you—I fed you with fine flour and oil and honey—you set before them for a pleasing aroma; and so it was, declares the Lord God. And you took your sons and your daughters, whom you had borne to me, and these you sacrificed to them to be devoured. Ezekiel 16:17-20

Let us run and give to our God what belongs to him! Let us keep the beautiful jewels of *his* gold and of *his* silver which he gave to us for him alone! Let us throw away the images of men, the brand names, the false identities, the worldly icons, and keep ourselves unstained from the world! Let us take our embroidered garments back and cover ourselves and stand once again in his grace! Let us no longer put *his* oil and *his* incense before dead and mute images, but cast them before the throne of the living and eternal one! Let us not give *his* bread to be trampled on by the world! And above all, let us not desert our sons and daughters, who belong to *him*, to the world's vicious and deceptive ways, but pursue them with love and forbearance to keep them healthy in the sheepfold of God!

9. We must be sober-minded.

...and there must be no filthiness and silly talk, or coarse jesting, which are not fitting, but rather giving of thanks. Ephesians 5:4

The key-note of your conversation should not be nastiness or silliness or flippancy, but a sense of all that we owe to God. Ephesians 5:4 Phillips

It is easy to kill the presence of the Spirit with flippant joking or foolish talking.[14] Believers who gather or assemble together ought to put away pointless and distracting thoughts or worries if they will experience the power and presence of the Holy Spirit who works through sensitive consciences and quiet spirits.

But I am afraid that as the serpent deceived Eve by his cunning, your thoughts will be led astray from a sincere and pure devotion to Christ. 2 Corinthians 11:3

While there is place and time for laughing and joking, there is place and time for sobriety. Wisdom will teach us when that time is and where that place is. Church should have some sort of "place" for seriousness, or "fear and trembling" (Psalm 2:11, Phil. 2:12), although laughing can certainly have its place in church as well. But we must have wisdom about what we're doing and why, which is the purpose of these scriptures.

For everything there is a season, and a time for every matter under heaven…a time to weep, and a time to laugh…a time to mourn, and a time to dance…a time to keep silence, and a time to speak… Ecclesiastes 3:1

The gathering is a time to focus on our identity as Christians eagerly awaiting the coming of our Kingdom in its fullness. We are "christian" at any given time of the day in any kind of gathering, but we are not always focused in that collective

---

[14] Ephesians 4:29-30

conscience. That is the point of gathering *in his name*. We gather not simply as friends, or as families, or as people with common interests or goals, but *as* children of God, *as* a royal priesthood, *as* a holy and spiritual nation, *as* citizens of the kingdom of heaven (1 Pet 2:9). It is then that our prayers reach the throne of God and Christ shows up! If we are awake we understand that we live in a state of fallenness and groaning out of which we fight for joy and have hope. If we are asleep we feel as though life is a state of joy and happiness out of which we must fight against suffering and discomfort. But,

...we know that the whole creation has been groaning together in the pains of childbirth until now. And not only the creation, but we ourselves, who have the firstfruits of the Spirit, groan inwardly as we wait eagerly for adoption as sons, the redemption of our bodies. Romans 8:22-23

The end of all things is at hand; therefore be self-controlled and sober-minded for the sake of your prayers. 1 Peter 4:7

10. We must understand our true identity.

Do you not know that you all are God's temple and that God's Spirit dwells in you all? If anyone destroys God's temple, God will destroy him. For God's temple is holy, and you all are that temple. 1 Corinthians 3:16-17

I betrothed you to one husband, to present you as a pure virgin to Christ. 2 Corinthians 11:2

The crucial point is whether God is pleased when we gather or not. When we gather for Jesus sake, we are collectively the Bride, or the Temple of God, in soul and spirit. How we act as such is the question then—are we being a whore or a beautiful bride? Are we trampling his courts or bowing our hearts in humility and fear? Are we grieving the Spirit or listening to what he has to say?

11. We must wait and keep watch together.

Our soul waits for the Lord; he is our help and our shield. Psalm 33:20

Bind up the testimony; seal the teaching among my disciples. I will wait for the Lord, who is hiding his face from the house of Jacob, and I will hope in him. Isaiah 8:16-17

So, could you not watch with me one hour? Watch and pray that you may not enter into temptation. The spirit indeed is willing, but the flesh is weak. Matthew 26:40-41

Somewhere along the line, the modern church dumped the prayer meeting and soon what was meant to be a sacred gathering quickly became a "service" in which we have found ourselves waiting upon people instead of upon the Lord. To still one's soul and wait on the Lord is to imply a deep relationship and fear of the Lord or going precisely toward that end. "Godliness is of value in every way, as it holds promise for the present life and also for the life to come…to this end we toil and strive…"[15]

For many, it would be ill-fitting, or their soul would be troubled, just to wait upon the Lord for it is precisely because he is holy and to be feared. He makes our flesh tremble in dread. God is near to the brokenhearted, and saves those of a contrite spirit. He is not known to rip open the heavens and come down on behalf of a coffee confab or a 15 minute "worship service". That is yet to be seen.

But the modern Christian trends are pulling the masses towards godless social club palavers. A place where anyone will feel comfortable, especially wolves in sheep's clothing. Pure devotion to Christ seems to have been twisted and geared toward our great American "pursuit of happiness". What I am not talking about is Christians doing fun things together, but about gathering as *church*. The crucial difference between that and any other kind of gathering is that you are searching out the face of God and not your own happiness.

But what happens when we scorn the practice of waiting on the Lord, or rousing ourselves to take a hold of God? Our faith fades like a leaf….and when we fade like a leaf, our sins, like wind take us away.[16]

Faith comes to those who listen, and listening to the word of the Lord, and that means *waiting on him.*

---

[15] 1 Timothy 4
[16] Isaiah 61:6-7

12. We must strive for unity in diversity.

America was never a cultural "melting pot" but rather more of a salad bowl. In some places you can actually find Somali refugees, blacks, whites, Hispanics, and Native Americans all living in the same neighborhood. What is amazing is the lack of mixing among Christians coming from different cultures and ethnic backgrounds. Indeed it seems too difficult to be a congregation of diverse cultures than to just be a congregation of one culture. Of course, it doesn't mean that the different cultures are unable to get along. But then what does it mean? Is not every Christian's identity found in one heavenly nation and royal kingdom?

But pick almost any city in America. The Koreans have their own church, the Chinese have their own church, the Africans-Americans have their own church, the Russians, the Arabs, the Messianic Jews, and so on. Why aren't they all found intermingling and breaking bread at the same table?

There is neither Jew nor Greek, there is neither slave nor free, there is no male and female, for you are all one in Christ Jesus. Galatians 3: 28

From this scripture we can get a sense of the unity that not only binds every believer in the body of Christ, but which also supersedes our earthly identities and affinities. In this sense it might be understood that there should be no problem for us to have multi-ethnic and multi-cultural congregations, and indeed there are some in existence. Yet there remains a very definite division in the body of Christ along the lines of cultural heritage. This very well may be due to a lack of conforming to the image of

Christ who is all, and in all, and through all. 2 Corinthians 5:17 says that the old person has passed and the new person has come. This verse is understood spiritually and means we are bound together by a common spiritual identity. The rest of our earthly nature, whether it is Asian or Latino, male or female, is still with us and so still defines us. It is God's design.[17]

The cup of blessing that we bless, is it not a participation in the blood of Christ? The bread that we break, is it not a participation in the body of Christ? Because there is one bread, we who are many are one body, for we all partake of the one bread. 1 Corinthians 10:16-17

But that the body of Christ should be divaricated according to heritage and culture does not seem to fulfill the purposes and glories of God. We are to "make every effort to keep the unity of the Spirit"[18] which means that we ought to be bringing each of our cultural heritages to one table for all to partake of. We are not supposed to abandon what God has given each of us nor try to change another peoples' culture. But American Christians are afraid of each other because we all come from so many different backgrounds. Therefore we need to come back to a genuine fear of God and stop fearing man, so that we can work together through the diversity God has graciously given to the American Church.

We must embrace these different glories in Christ, who is the redeemer of culture, the redeemer of man and woman, and in whom we are spiritually neither male nor female, White nor

---

[17] Psalm 139:14
[18] Ephesians 4:3

Black, white collar nor blue collar. There is only one table. Let's learn to share it.

There is but One Thing Necessary

Filled with empty tasks and overcome with anxiety
Her heart is debauched with the wine of yesterday's agendas,
tomorrow's plans, today's hopes
Her face is low and cumbersome to look at.
The pace of her work is multiplied into ignorance
As the sun rises and vents its clandestine gleam upon her
It glances off of her back; she is turned away in the darkness of her
task

What task, what approval, what accomplishment is written
That could be likened to the contract of blood made in ancient of
days
Made to accomplish what cannot be accomplished
Made to create what cannot be created?

What word, what deed, what success
Can meet the measure of your Fathers request?
This collage of hand shaking, dedicating, certificating, accumulating
Is a dying tree cluttered with the ornaments of death!

Distractions and hopes behind picture frames
Faithfulness and devotion to the dust and the flies
Complaints and grievances on those who do not accumulate
She equates her master's favor in the multiplication, subtraction, and
division of time

Light is warm and becoming; she sees her sister is enamored
But there is little regard in her eyes for that one
She is desperate for a better image, a better status

Manipulation, vice, emotional condescension; how clenched is her heart!

Can she not see the better portion?
The proven and finished work?
Are her eyes glazed with the stains of promotion?
O faithless daughter!
How long will you slumber on the scales of production?
Freedom cries out at the gates!
Will you not let her in?

Martha, Martha, O my American Daughter!
Where is the salve to relinquish your hidden troubles?
Your children are crying in the streets!
Relieve me of the equations and absurd schedules of pomp and circumstance!
Let down the apron of your distress, and come!
Cast off the agendas of pride and self-sufficiency, O Daughter of maldevelopment!
Come out from behind the picture frames, come sit; turn your face!
Remove the veil and behold the warmth of the gleam
which was cast forth for you from days of old!
Seek the better way, the way of the One!
For there is "but one thing necessary"!

Made in the USA
Charleston, SC
13 April 2010